To
Friends @
Wilcox Winery for
Thanks you
US.

MW00932542

IN MY
Shoes

A Walk Toward Independent Faith

DAWN FELDMAN-STEIS

iUniverse

IN MY SHOES
A WALK TOWARD INDEPENDENT FAITH

iUniverse books may be ordered through booksellers or by contacting:

iUniverse
1663 Liberty Drive
Bloomington, IN 47403
www.iuniverse.com
844-349-9409

ISBN: 978-1-6632-2089-9 (sc)
ISBN: 978-1-6632-2088-2 (hc)
ISBN: 978-1-6632-2090-5 (e)

Library of Congress Control Number: 2021908712

Print information available on the last page.

iUniverse rev. date: 04/28/2021

In Loving Memory of
Maryann Kunselman
"I just did it"

Dedicated to my Mom
Penelope Feldman
"It's an easy obligation to be called your daughter,
And an absolute privilege to call you friend."

Special Thanks to
Georgette Tsongos
Lotus photography

My kick ass editor
Wendy Ruth Walker

Most importantly, thank you to everyone mentioned or supportive
to this project. All the impacts both negative
and positive have made this possible.
So, a big thank you for pushing me to step forward
in courage, no matter the influence.

The Start of It

I have wanted to write a book for some time regarding the abusiveness of religion and its ability to control without question, those who chose to believe. To examine this indoctrination within belief systems and why it is so very devastating to so many. I have taken a good long look at it and looking back through my own years and experiences I see a commonality emerge in the stories, that should not go unnoticed. It starts in the very hearts of the leadership. I have come to believe that religion as well as the original sin stem from co-dependency. In order to better understand this and to come into a thought pattern of independent belief I decided to share how I became independent in my own beliefs. You will have to figure out how to apply it to your own.

First and most importantly we should understand this word co-dependence. I mean for generations this word has been thrown around. It's been used to defined addicts and those that support addicts of all addictions. It's been used to excuse behavior in mental health and abusive behavior patterns. But what is it really? Here is the definition… "Codependency is a behavioral condition in a relationship where one person enables another person's addiction, poor mental health, immaturity, irresponsibility, or under achievement. Among the core characteristics of codependency is an excessive reliance on other people for approval and a sense of identity. "(Wiki) This all sounds awfully bad and codependency at is core is very bad, but what if it is much more subtle in its manipulations of people. What if we look at being codependent not as a behavior or condition of behavior but what if we define it as something within our capacity that limits our understanding of emotion and our connections to those things that matter most. Our capacity as humans is endless. WE are all creators and use our imaginations to gain and grow and in doing so our capacity grows bigger and farther. So here are my thoughts before we move forward into my personal journey.

I believe that codependence is not part of our abilities but lies within our capacity as humans. That we are capable of many things and though many people might say that we are codependent, it just is part of the human condition, it does not have to be true. That independence is not only an idea it is possible in all relationships we have whether they be personal or material. I am choosing to expose these ideas by way of how religious leaders have kept people from genuinely believing independently and personally within their chosen religion for a couple reasons. One reason is that it has led me to become a minister to show a different idea in the concept of belief and two people do not have to continue to be abused by wanting and knowing a higher power.

When it comes to religion and religious leaders, anyone wanting that buy in has a choice to manipulate the knowledge of codependent behavior or to promote self-thinkers within that belief system. What Religious leaders have yet to recognize, is that the churches will continue to grow without their leadership, in both self-thought and independent belief. That many people who have left the churches have done so in self-preservation to the god force inside them telling them there is more than what is being said in the four walls of organized religion.

Understanding the labels and the need for them, within the capacity of codependence gives us a new insight into what it takes to be an independent believer and lover of God and all of creation. We spend our lifetimes searching for our personal labels. Where do I belong and fit in. What label will bring me the most acceptance into the whole of it and the group. Just think about the limits we place on ourselves daily and more importantly how those labels define our actions and capacities of becoming more. Christian, Jew, Muslim, Buddhist, etc. LGBTQ, Republican democrat liberal conservative... When we accept anyone label as our definition or a piece to our definition, we place ourselves in a position to operate in the stereotypes of those labels. We create a capacity to operate codependently to the label accepted and we lock ourselves in for that ride. The problem with rides is they almost always have a beginning and an end and that means they, no matter how squiggly a loop or circle, are causing us to repeat our choices over and over in cycles, and cycles limit capacity and magnify codependency.

We have been designed and created to be free thinkers with unlimited abilities to create and imagine. What would happen if we made a conscious effort to retrain the subconscious being to accept all labels? What if we woke up tomorrow and said to ourselves, I am Muslim, Christian, Buddhist? I am LGBTQ, I am democrat republican socialist communist... I am a tyrant and free thinker, a liar and honest, poor and prosperous. To accept all labels instead of limiting them brings us into a different kind of thought. It opens our capacities to be independent because we have defined ourselves as everything we experience and if we define ourselves to those things, we most hate, how can we continue to hate them? Accepting all labels as one's self gives us a unique opportunity to promote creativity, development and growth and it projects the original connectiveness and love of God into the present. It eliminates the connections of the past and the dreams of the future and places us right here right now. It shows us the full potential as beloved creatures of an ever-present God in all of creation and that we are all connected to that one source without limitations.

I have been hurt and watched others get hurt over and over by the acceptance of labels and trying to live up to those standards with in them. That accepting only part of the whole can cripple and disfigure the spirit. I can only share my own stories of these things that hurt so deeply in the hope that they might reflect the pain of others and give the knowledge that it can change, and we can believe outside of the rules of a label by taking ownership of all labels. I chose to do this through my experiences in organized religion because understanding that outcome is becoming free, and I think it is time for folks to have permission to question the leaders within the message. As a minister myself I want to be questioned. I want the message I bring today to be added to tomorrow by your thoughts and your message. I want the love I have come to know to be understood and magnified by the folks listening. I want to bring some understanding to the questions I have wrestled with, with the hope that it will help another. I want to expose the what if...

What if independence and our ability to embrace it comes from our capacity to align ourselves with each other?

Contents

Contents

The Confusion of the Church Child

"Fear and Faith cannot occupy the same space."

C hurch, Temple, Synagogue etc. All of these are interesting concepts that I have come to believe Jesus himself would struggle with and did struggle with. Yes, I do see how important it can be for the building of foundations of belief, but I have also witnessed the destruction that this can cause to individuals and whole families alike, and it is the very reason that I have finally stepped forward to write this book. The only way I can get to the amazement I have found in the church in my later years is to go backward first, and share a few experiences of church as a child, a sensitive child at that, under a rigid indoctrination of faith and belief, and more importantly fear.

I come from a small knock about town in northern Pennsylvania. Rich in history and beauty. It is one of those nostalgic places that seems like a postcard from wonderful memories and relaxing times. One thing this small town and its neighboring towns was not short of, was churches. My hometown alone had 10 operational churches at one time, many of which, now, are being sold off as housing and new business ideas today. That little fact alone infers to the issues I intend to address in this book concerning the church today and its transformation. Out of the churches available, my family was Episcopalian. I was baptized as per the tradition at three or four years of age at Grace Church in Ridgway. Grace church has got to be one of the most beautiful places on earth to me. Its ornate wood carvings and picturesque stain glass windows feel like a giant hug every time I chance to take a seat under them. The church is an absolutely stunning attribute to the town, and a show of adornment to a God who is so loved and embraced by this faith. The walls exude reverence and even today you can *almost* still smell the faint hint of incense that has soaked within the wood as a reminder to all our senses that God is with us and in us always.

When my mother became a Christian and we started back to church stuff, I became terrified, yes from age four on I would be gripped by fears so deep that sometimes they would cause my body to cramp in the middle of the night. As a young child I spent many nights sleeping in my mother's bed. I remember waking up and laying there working up the courage to run the small distance through our apartment from my room to my mothers. Sometimes she would take me back to bed, but I would just end back up with her again. At the time I only knew that I was afraid, and she was my mom. Enough said. Looking back on it my fear was very real and placed there by religion and the beliefs surrounding it. You see as I was being molested on a regular basis, yet, at the same time, being taught that sex outside of marriage was wrong, that hell was an eternal separation from God and loved ones. Given this, I automatically knew I was bound for hell. And yes, I had the clarity at that age to put it all together. This was discussed in my family because my mother was in a relationship and questioned her relationship outside of marriage. She would begin to question the safety of everything as it pertained to God versus eternal damnation. I figured if I stayed close enough to my all believing mother and kept an eye on her and kept her safe, I would somehow be spared from this painful demise. My fears would eventually, during my teen years, lead to anger and hate for the very God that would see me through them.

Dawn Feldman-Steis

Understanding that I was going to hell no matter what, because some other person decided to be inappropriate made me a bit defiant in Sunday school. About this time the two local churches began sharing a priest for a time, one week at our church the next week in a neighboring town. The Sunday school teacher, at the away church didn't really like children, or at least that was my opinion of her. She would tell us stories using those paper dolls attached to the felt board, you know where Johnny and Sue could go up and place the doll on the board as if it was some sort of reward. I was having none of that. I could see right through that paper doll trap. Instead, I would ask questions. Why did they throw Joseph in the hole? Why would they even have a lion's den to put people in? I sat many of Sunday mornings in the art supply closet, which was just fine with me. That time out closet was a mixed bag for me, it was great that I was away from Sunday school, but it separated me from my mother, and I could not see her and that always made for a load of anxiety for me, because she was my only ticket into heaven. The time out closet ended after one Sunday when they went off to church and forgot me in there. I used the time to get acquainted with the new coloring books (all of them) and crayons. I am pretty sure I colored in every book on that shelf. It felt like a long time, but my mother came and got me, and I was never put back in there again. I often chuckle and wonder, in retrospect, what the conversation was surrounding putting me in that closet between my mother and the teacher? And more importantly forgetting about me and heading off to church? What I most definitely took away from that experience was that you cannot and should not question the church leaders. It really pisses them off. So, of course, I would do just that whenever the opportunity came.

I remember in 1978 we went to Jesus '78 Festival weekend. Jesus' festivals were a three-day camping adventure for church groups and Christians alike to attend. We'd gathered in a big open field somewhere in central PA. My mom always made things sound so exciting even if she herself had no idea what we were getting into. We didn't travel outside of town much when we were young as mom did not have a vehicle so when she got a chance to take us somewhere, she was all in and we were convinced to be just the same. For whatever reason, our family felt it best we attend in '78, and we went with the Sunday School teacher. Yep, this woman was very much like my grandmother, they loved you hard with a stern hand and the care of teaching you things with the abrasiveness of heavy-duty sandpaper. What on earth and in all the heavens where my family members thinking? Why would we attend a weekend with someone that put me in a closet and forgot I was there?! And furthermore, my grandmother and camping were probably not a good idea. There are only two things I remember about that weekend. I remember the Sunday School teacher losing her patience with me yet again, simply because I was more than upset that my mother had gone off to listen to a preacher and didn't take me with her. The teacher would pick me up and slam me down twice very hard onto the tail hitch of the camper, and again in time out, but the pain of being slammed down was so intense that it was all I could do to stay seated. The pain shot up my spine and my small legs tingled. I cried very loud and very long. I was a tiny kid, maybe all of twenty-five pounds at age six. Again, my mother and hero would show up out of nowhere and I remember her voice stating sternly, "What have you done to my Dawn Marie?" She would always say that when someone had hurt me. She would pick me up and spend the next half hour calming me down. I was with her the rest of the weekend and never left her side. The other thing I remember about our weekend of everything God was getting a blessing from a well-known minister. My mom explained that we were going to get some prayer and we all gathered and stood in a line across the field. This preacher guy would start at one end of the line and pray for each person moving his way down the line. As this guy lifted his hand to touch folks they just fell over, and I was like umm, what's happening?! I felt a knot forming in my throat as my mouth became dry, and immense fear began to weaken my legs. My first thought was... Oh shit, he is killing people with prayer! Maybe God knows of our sins and wrongs, and when this guy touches us, we die, and they are all just dying right here, right now. I am sure my mother felt my grip tighten as the minister got closer. I recall my mother grabbing both my sister and I a bit harder and she sat down onto the ground on her own before he got to us, pulling us down with her. Phew! Saved again from whatever the hell that was! My mother and I have talked about that since and she explained that she felt that the minster was forcing people to the ground as a way to show the movement of the spirit (what fundamentalists call Slain in the spirit) she didn't feel this was appropriate for her or us to be a part of at the time, so she made certain to sit us down. She was quick to inform us that the holy spirit can work great wonders, but we must learn to discern between the wants of people versus the desires of God. What the hell were my liturgical Episcopal people thinking when they attended a bible thumping fundamental weekend event? I have to laugh about it now, those quiet purposed liturgical Episcopalians spending the weekend with loud obnoxious evangelicals and not a bottle of gin or vodka in sight... that's material for a stand-up show, that is. That weekend God became death, and I was locked into the capacity of fear that went with this.

In fourth grade I was pulled out of public school for the next couple years as a new Baptist PACE school had opened and my family, along with other families from the town's churches thought it best to send us there for a bit. ACE schooling worked on a merit system using PACE curriculum. The school was like a Montessori school slammed into religion and Bam. I remember we had to go and interview with the pastor just to get into this place. My mother, my sister and I all sat down in the church, which was a trailer at the time. That should have been a screaming warning sign, but instead, we began discussing why we would want to attend this program. Of course, I said nothing and was accepted. My sister? Well, she literally sat there and ate the bottom of her tennis shoe off while the shoe was still on her foot and they said, after witnessing this act of crazy, "We are not going to allow your oldest daughter to attend. Due to her behavior, we just cannot accept her into this school at this time." They may have suggested some sort of exorcism for her as well, lol, I know I would have. I remember my mom mumbling to her as we got in the car, asking my sister what was wrong with her and how embarrassing to have a child eat their sneaker in an interview. Looking back, it was absolutely genius, I mean what church group wants a possessed kid running around, it's just bad for business. Lol! PACE stood for Packet of Accelerated Christian Education. Ok so that sucked, *and* they made me wear a uniform, of course a dress. We had to cross our legs a certain way, pray a certain way, read only one chosen translation of the bible and the pastor was a big ole asshole. He once sat and watched us have a snowball fight. He wrote on a piece of paper a tally of how many snowballs each child threw. When we came back inside, he had the teachers stand us in a line to the office to receive a smack for each ball thrown. I remember standing toward the back of the line not really understanding what was happening. Then as each child went into the office alone, they would come back out, walk down the thin trailer hallway crying or with tears in their eyes. When I got about third in line, I suddenly realized this was not a good meeting I was about to have and there was absolutely no way out. I walked into the room and there sat the pastor perched behind his desk, looking somewhat humored with himself. His wife walked over and stood beside me and he said, "Dawn you are called into this office today for throwing 8 snowballs and throwing snowballs is against the rules, is it not? You will receive one whack for each snowball thrown. Since I am a man and stronger than a girl, my wife will provide the discipline to you today." I looked up at her and then back at him. He continued, "If you should cry before we get to eight, I will spare you the rest. Your tears will show and prove that you learned a lesson about breaking the rules." They had me bend over and place my hands on a child's desk in front of him so he could watch and count as she did his bidding, 1, 2, 3, and so on. Each one felt a little harder a little stronger as if they wanted me to cry out. But I did not. I would not be learning any lesson today. I stood my ground. I stood up after she hit 8 and faced him with only a bit of a tear welling in my eyes. He looked at me intently and said, "Just cry let it go." I defiantly for the first time ever said, "NO!" He proceeded to sentence me to two more whacks by his own hand. They were angry and strong blows, but I stood again and faced him with not one tear to release. Oh, they were there but I didn't blink, I did not give him any satisfaction to break me. I did not give him the part me that matter to him the most, he could not take my spirit from me. I remember walking down the hall, and for the first time, as I walked it felt as if with each step, I was pulling up, from deep within, pieces of hard shell and as I walked, I began to place it around me as a sort of armor. Like every step forward another patch of shell would be added so that by the time I got to the end of the hall the tears just sitting there ready to fall had dried up. Suddenly I found an invisible protection that said no one is going to hurt me anymore. All the folks that hurt me before this moment and those to come, I was clear of them. I had found this new emotion that would protect me through anything, with 10 whacks and a long walk down that trailer hall, as I took that very last step, I felt rage. A rage so deep and hot that it burned up any chance of me shedding another tear, ever, and would carry me well into my young twenties.

They would shut the school down the following year due to low attendance and I was sent back to public school by the end of the fifth-grade school year.

It was about this time that the Episcopal church split. There seemed to be some nonsense about the prayer books and the hymnals as well as a women's role in the church. Father John was the current priest and the first religious leader I could really look up to. He seemed so tall and handsome to me as a child, but to see him now he's not so tall. He believed in the role of women serving in the church as more than just choir members or alter guild. He made certain to act in his belief as well. My sister and I were the first girls to serve as acolytes on the alter at Grace. It was finally something that made church worth attending and it was interactive for me. I remember while getting our robes on one Sunday looking at Father John and saying, "I wanna be just like you and run a church." He bent down with all the realism he could muster and said, "I fear that will never be able to happen for you." I interpreted that as if he was saying I didn't have what it takes, but what he was saying, really, was that he didn't think women would win the fight to serve in the church. He was a good man, that Father John was, and will always hold a special place for me. He is the example of strength in simple faith to me still. The church split, and my family left Grace and we began attending Faith church.

Talk about a culture change.

Faith United Church of Christ was a fundamentalist church on the west end of town. It had a sizable youth group and plenty of Holy Spirit to go around for non-Christian and Christian alike. There was singing and dancing and public shows of praise and worship. Folks would speak in tongues without hesitation, and everyone was on fire for God all the time, whatever that meant. The only thing separating them from the Pentecostals was that we didn't have snakes. It was all very strange and odd to me to make

God such a circus and to attempt to define him as fun and carefree? I couldn't help but wonder what was wrong with these folks? I was, honestly, insulted by the lack of reverence. I was pushed to be confirmed in the church at age 14, which was so disappointing. That it would have to be at Faith United. I figured I'd do it to please my family and it wouldn't hurt to assure my passage into heaven but, just wow.

It was around this time that my mom had fully incorporated her beliefs and her relationship with God as a co-parent for her children. Each single parent does this, we all find some belief or thing to help us with parenting when other parents are absent. My mom chose religion, which is not so bad when you think of the alternatives. It could have been alcohol or drugs as a co-parent. It could have been physical abuse or just absence period. But for me and my sister it was God. So of course, if God is placed as your father and the co-parenting companion of choice then it would not be but a couple years before I was in complete rebellion to God. Right? I mean who hasn't rebelled in their own way against their parents and their parents parenting techniques. Isn't it a fundamental part of being a teenager, a true rite of passage? the obvious next step was to get really angry with my mom and angry with God. I mean if God was my father and with what I witnessed of him; he was an abusive father, full of vengeance and hate and wanting to find ways to send you to hell. There was no mercy in this father, no grace or love, just fear and eternal damnation if it wasn't his way. So why not get angry with God before he can set his goals of damnation toward me?

By age fifteen fear finally won, as the true driving force in my life. I lost both, my grandfather to cancer and my father to a bar fight. Any hope of male influence outside of God the father was gone to me. It was in this time I just could not bear the constant fear of eternal damnation and a forever fiery death. I left it all behind me and picked up smoking, drinking and drugging as a much better alternative. At least I felt I was making my own choices and living my best independent life. Thank God, all of us, that had praying parents to keep us all alive during informative years.

Looking back and for the purposes of seeing the point. I really believe it's so important to know this kind of family history as it speaks to where we are headed in the journey of this book and the journey that has already been walked. I have learned that the co-dependence of religion starts very early for many children. God is not explained as a God of mercy and kindness, as a loving father or mother. All these years later, I look at what I went through growing up and feel so strongly that we must stop scaring people into faith—the two things cancel each other out and separate us from our own divine spirit with in. God and the spirit cannot work together in tandem if the mind is in constant battle with the spirit. The mind will surely educate the spirit over time, and too many times I have witnessed churches putting folks to sleep rather than building them up to have independent partnerships with both God and the God force with in themselves. So many things have stuck with me over the years.

I have talked with people that wouldn't read outside of the 66 books of the bible, as they had been taught that the bible should not be altered in any way. Someone else believed that the King James Bible represents the only real word of God. I had a pastor friend tell me once that he couldn't teach outside of the 66 books as folks didn't know of the other holy books. I can't help but look at that for a moment. I mean the bible was not put together until the fifth century, so that means that not one person writing the scriptures wrote their texts with the hopes of them being placed together in one book. They did not ring each other up and say hey let's all get together and write a book. Yes, in the book of revelation, John states "take nothing from this and add nothing to it", meaning his book, the one he was writing. Those that wrote the bible had no way of knowing what would come of their texts let alone imagine it would influence more than 2000 plus years of doctrine. I've come to believe, and my childhood has been the foundation of this thinking, that we should attempt to read all the holy texts, the omitted books as well as the Torah and Koran, any text that brings fragments of the whole back together. God is a God of spirit and truth not a God of knowledge. Humans are a people of knowledge; we feel we must know something to believe something, and yet the only way to truly know something is to study everything. Part of my writing this book is to suggest that we study all things with discernment and through prayer, its ok! If this seems hard, start with the books of the bible that have been left out, Adam and Eve, Enoch, Jasher, or start with the small texts of the Torah or Koran that have been omitted, and so on. You may just find that those things left out encourage and confirm the love and grace of God and show you a more open belief then the legalism of the 66 books we have been handed. Folks don't know all of God's word because we are not teaching all of the word. If you have been sitting in a church setting for more than two years and you have not been encouraged to look into all the holy texts, then you are being complacent in your beliefs and choosing to stay young. We must grow, we must learn, and we must gain the courage to step forward to define and begin our own ministries.

Co-dependency depends greatly on complacency in our capacity as humans. If you attend your place of worship as a way to get by or because it's the right thing to do, or you think this is how we get to eternal coexistence with God, you are wrong. If your beliefs are tied to four walls and relics and nothing more, you are in muddy waters. If you have been abused by leadership in the church and struggle to stand up to it or state your discernment of the matter, if you are fearful of your leadership, then I suggest and give you permission to question the church and the leadership. If you genuinely care about the folks you sit next to and the leaders of your place of worship, I ask you to step courageously and ask questions, ask for explanation and dialog. You have every permission to ask questions of the church and you are worth the answers. Not doing so will keep us bound to an ideal of control and sameness. At what point have you ever looked at creation and seen it the same twice. That tree across the field changes daily as well as through the seasons. Change is a wheel within a wheel and is it infinitely free. Embracing the constant in church walls is accepting a co-dependent belief, and our faith and beliefs are not meant to be locked down. They are meant to force us to continue to create and force a larger capacity within ourselves to be independent.

I am abusive and led by my own ego at times, but I am understanding and kind. What if understanding itself is the acceptance of others beliefs as genuine to them, that staying the same or being the same weakens our capacities to create and limits our ability to be kind? The outcome of limiting our ability to create and imagine is codependence. Finding a new independent foundation causes us to step forward, ask questions, to be brave. It's the start of finding a new way to breath, in the stagnant air of traditional beliefs.

Dawn Feldman-Steis

John's Angel

*"God sends his angels when they are
most needed and least noticed.*

"My father and mother were just kids out of high school
when they got married; my mother, pregnant with her
first child, did what was expected at the time and married my dad.
My father was, even then, a heavy drinker and my mother was
looking to rebel from the strict environment in her childhood home
and was satisfied to use both John's drinking and his reputation
to piss her own mother off. And yet they would lose the baby that
brought them together, and this would send John deeper down the
hole with drinking and partying, and leave my mother to mourn in
her own way. So began their marriage. Two kids later and six years
down the road my father and mother decided, or I should say my
mother decided that divorce was the only option, and it was time to
end the relationship. I was between eighteen months and two years
old when they got divorced. I knew nothing of their relationship
and even less about my father. I never really felt the void of not
having my father in my life. You have to know something to miss
something. I am very sure that my sister felt a loss when my father
and mother split, and if she were to be honest, she probably still feels
that loss today. However, through the years I would come to know
my father through different lenses and the power of hindsight.

My father came from a family of co-dependents, as in they all
had their time with drinking and some with drugs and they all

13

ensured each other assistance in continued use of these things. Dad was born a twin, and his sister would pass away as an infant leaving him to be my grandmother's only son. My dad's mother, we called her Grandma Lover, had eleven pregnancies and births but only saw to raise two children out of the lot. These losses, I believe, caused deep pain for my grandparents and gave them a reason to hold fast to their addictions as a way to numb those pains. Addiction really does not leave much for kids growing up trying to understand why, even though both parents lived under the same roof with them, they still feel so separated from the whole of the family. Needless to say, my dad and his older sister would struggle with these feelings of absence when they both needed to feel loved and tucked in.

Eventually my dad became a drinker just like his parents, and a good one at that. On the Feldman side we always go big and work off the moto of, if you are going to do something do it right. Dad's drinking would lead him through life with continued losses, wives would come and go, girlfriends too, but drinking remained. My mother told him he could see us at any time but he had to come sober. He would lose time with his daughters and yet drinking remained, so in-depth his pain that it was more comfortable to drink then to take notice to what and who he was missing. I pondered once if he ever recognized what he was hiding all the years he drank. I would pause to think that if he got to know us, he would come more often, and the next drink would not matter as much.

We did not see my father often due to the rules set by my mother, but he would pop in here and there for a few hours on a holiday or birthday, but never stayed long and mostly brought gifts that my mother could never afford for us and then be gone as quickly as he came. Then, in early Spring of '85, the year I turned thirteen, my dad wrote to my mother. In his very long letter, he explained that he was sitting in a local bar having his after-work

Dawn Feldman-Steis

drinks, hanging with his buddies telling tales and living the lie of a good life that you can only understand if you spend a majority of your time in a bar listening to other folk's stories. In the letter he spoke of sitting there having his beer when, this guy who he had never met and had never known sat down beside him. The gentleman never introduced himself, but began talking to my dad and told him things that he had done that no one should had ever known. He talked with him about his life and how he was not living. At the end of a two-hour conversation, this man told my dad that if he did not quit drinking, he would die, and that his life would not be remembered by anyone. The man insisted my father would be utterly lost to this life and would leave no legacy to be remembered in the bottle he'd learned to trust. The letter continued with my dad telling us he was currently in rehab and had been sober for well over a month. He requested not only forgiveness for his past mistakes but that he see us girls and start to build relationships with both my sister and me. My mother did not read the letter to us until the day my father actually came to visit for the first time. After his visit she would read us the letter he had sent earlier in the year and explain that she wanted us to know that he is trying, but she had to be sure before putting us into the position of being hurt by his absence or another broken promise. She sat that night and read the story of the man who brought John back to trying and living sober.

By early summer dad was sober and invested in getting to know his kids. He came to see us when he wasn't working. He worked more days and longer hours to keep busy and his mind focused on being a new man. He would spend time with us and always take a moment to make a pass at my mom, hoping maybe he could patch things up and start over, always answered by a flattered giggle and a prompt no. He would talk with me about the man he met and how it changed him. His energy was new and changed, he appeared freer, lighter. But dad still struggled, every day, he was still bound to the rage and anger and the fears that drove him to drink all those years. What was this magical force that kept him so tied to the past? As much as he changed his life, he could not figure out how to let go of the things that really mattered, he did not know how to quit his emotions. I saw the struggle deep in his eyes, in that part where the soul lives. I saw the hurt and despair and longing for acceptance and approval and the fear to ask for it. I knew that soul as if it was my twin, but I also knew how to quit the emotion of it all, I knew how to be numb without self-medication, or at least I thought I did.

John and I had a good two years of visits, and getting to know each other. Swimming and walking to the park, just talking or hanging out our apartment window watching the annual town parade and picking on folks that walked by. It felt good to know him, to laugh with him to know he was trying. In February 1987, my dad called and explained that he would have to miss our plans for the upcoming weekend. My mom took the call and I overheard her saying no John you will tell her; she wasn't going to make excuses for him. So, when I took the phone and my dad told me he was not going to make it, I questioned him. I asked if he was drinking again. He said no. He explained that he had met someone and was going to be doing something with her and he would come the following weekend. I said it was ok, but I knew when I hung up the phone that I would not be spending anymore weekends with dad. Our weekends were over, I just knew. I had lost my grandfather a few weeks before this, and he was my one true friend and love in my family. It was hard to let him go and now my father was heading back to his old life, his old ways. It was all so suddenly real and devastating, but I had rage to help me through it all—it was my escape from the rawness of this new way of feeling rejection.

The weekend that dad and I were to get together came and went. There was no word from him not even a call and as quickly as he came into my life he was gone. Then, on Sunday, March 6th to be exact, a call came in. It was my grandmother. I heard low voices and my mother trying to understand, as she asked further questions of my Grandmother. She hung up the phone and gathered my sister and I and sat us down, as she would when it was time for one of her 'come to Jesus' talks. She explained that dad had been in an accident and had been sent by life flight to the Pittsburgh shock trauma center. She wasn't sure of any further information, but she explained that she would make sure to find out everything she could as soon as she could.

"What kind of accident?" I asked, "Was he drinking?"

Mom as reserved as possible said, "Yes, he was drinking, and he got into a bar fight with one of his friends and banged his head. I really don't know more than that."

I sat quietly thinking as quickly as I could as I felt myself swallow, my throat quivering and dry. With all the courage I owned I asked, "Will he die?"

I suddenly found myself thinking back to the last hug he gave me, the pressure of it how it felt like he was gonna hold on forever; how he whispered 'I love you' in my ear as if he knew in some small way that he wasn't coming back. He took extra time during that visit before leaving.

Turned out Dad had suffered a severe head injury. He was in a coma when we arrived at Shock Trauma. We were told that they were not certain what the outcome would be. My grandmother was not willing to let go of her only son and again she was faced with losing yet another child and this time one that she had grown to love deeply. She would do whatever it took to keep John alive and that they did.

I remember walking into the room that day. He looked as if he was sleeping, tubes coming from every part of his body. There were some machines to help him breathe, some to help him eat and more to help control his body temperature. The nurse was more than willing to answer any questions we had, even if we hadn't asked any. I refused to touch him; I did not want to run the risk of feeling how trapped he was in his own body. His story of the man in the bar telling him his life would be over if he continued to drink came rushing back. The echoes of my mother talking with my dad about how she thought that the man was God giving him a chance at amends. Was this the outcome of my dad choosing alcohol over me? God's punishment for my dad not heeding his warning? My heart was crushed, and I was so lost in it all. I was brought back to the room out of my deep thought by machines going off and them asking us to leave the room. I found myself getting all armored up with anger and rage, and I knew my trusted friends would protect me from anything. There were no tears, and by the end of that first visit I had managed to stuff any feelings I had for my father deep inside where they could not be seen or stolen away, protected and safe. When we drove away my mother said a brief prayer. She said, "God please do not take John home until he is right with you!" she continued to pray that same prayer for the six years he fought to accept his new way of life as disabled. He would never speak or walk again. Learning things like feeding himself became an exercise in family cheers and that a boys. All fine motor skills lost as his muscles began to atrophy.

With dad and my grandfather both being gone it made my Fifteenth year of life drastically difficult and I struggled with just about everything. School sucked, people in general were assholes and outside of my gang of friends I really had no time for the human race at all. God was back in full force as my father, my mother and I fought daily. I began using drugs and drinking, like a lot of teens my age living in my area. I kind of felt that it was a teenager's job to live life on the edge of death most days, and I lived to the fullest of that. I was a depressed and fearful kid and really had a harder and harder time in finding a center in my life. I relied heavily on music and had to smuggle secular music into the house and listen when mom and God weren't home. Had it not been for kick ass singers like Pat Benatar and Jan Krist I do not think I would have found a steady stance to just keep walking. To this day Jan's song "Wing and a Prayer" always comes to my mind when the struggles get real and the soul needs comfort.

At sixteen my sister and I were asked to sign papers that would make us the legal guardian of the person of our father, along with my grandmother, who would take on the guardianship of the property for him. Dad was being moved from Pittsburgh Rehab to Leer Medical Center in Erie, PA, where he would be woken from his deep sleep. He had been in a coma all this time. It was finally time to attempt to wake him. He would fight and live or fly and die.

Dad through a long process of routine exercises and removing medications, would eventually wake up, and when he did, boy he was pissed! He was no longer able to talk, but his eyes and face said it all. My mom was with us on the first visit, and he was so pissed at her, like he could not figure out why she had not been there before that moment. My mom talked to him and explained that she had not been there before now because they had been divorced for some time before he got hurt and that they were no longer husband and wife. He seemed to calm a bit as if someone played a lost part of a movie for him and he was able to remember. My mother was always good at picking up on emotions of folks and understanding why they were feeling them. She talked with dad briefly about using this time to get to know God and that he was in this position for a reason. While she spoke with him I began to replay the events in my head. I couldn't help but question God's motives. I mean, he was told by some stranger not to drink and he drank, and now his life is all fucked up. Was this the measure of Gods Angels? Was this God at his finest? My dad wouldn't have wanted to be kept alive if he knew we had that choice, which we did have at one point, but my grandmother simply could not let him go, so here we all were with a dad fully aware stuck in a body that would no longer work the same way. He could not talk, his legs atrophied along with his arms, and simple motor skills would need to be relearned. Until then he would have to be fed and changed and have everything done for him. What hell had he unwillingly entered by picking up a drink after so long? In the years that followed, there were struggles and fights to get and keep him home under nursing care, or at least closer to home. But it was an enormous struggle for all of us and dad was eventually placed in a smaller nursing facility in Erie, and there he would stay.

Visits with dad were a mixed bag. It would be great to spend a day with my father's side of the family as I didn't really know them well and it gave me time to learn who they were. I was always excited to see him, but then crushed with the burden of how incredibly trapped he was, how he seemed to be so angry and stuck. It was hard to watch. My mother would remind us and insist that dad was not going anywhere until he made things right with God. That was her prayer, and she was sticking to it. But for me, it made the rage inside flare and burn so deep that Father God would hold my father prisoner like some jealous new husband.

There was this one visit, though, that changed everything I knew about everything. My grandmother, cousin and I decided one Saturday to go visit dad; it was the typical start of a visit, trying to locate the clothing that was sent to him, finding spoiled towels in his drawers, clothes that weren't his, complaints being made to staff, and questions being asked of management, and so on. Meanwhile, I was sitting watching the college football game with dad and commenting on Penn state vs. the Mountaineers. I cut a joke about Penn State losing and my dad began to laugh. He laughed so hard he started to choke, as would happen due to the tracheotomy hole left in his throat from years before. He continued to laugh and choke, and as I busied myself folding some clothes, I told him he best calm it down a bit, or he'd die of laughing too much. Well, that got him laughing again. I paused and looked up. As I looked across the room, I caught his eyes, for the first time in a long time. I looked directly in his eyes as he was laughing. As he started to slow his laugh to a stop, I continued to watch him, and it felt as if everything in the moment had slowed down. I saw no hurt, no anger, no rage. Everything I knew of him that made us father and daughter was gone? I saw a light about him, a gleam of true joy in his eyes like a fresh baby or new spring kitten, a clear-eyed innocence staring back at me. My dad was healed, he had forgiven, he was forgiven, and he was transformed to the person he was always intended to be. Looking back, I feel as if, in that moment, I met my dad for the first time, and recognized the grace and forgiveness of God, and believed, with all of who I was, that my two dads had met each other, and they were together just as my mother prayerfully requested. The brightness and love that was in my father's eyes was shining and pure I could only look for a few moments and then had to look away, as I felt it would break me. It felt like the embrace in his eyes would somehow tear down my walls and he would see me as clearly as I was seeing him.

That evening I sat in the back seat of the car and just enjoyed the ride home. I watched the sun start to set and wondered if maybe dad looked at me so intently for a reason. Maybe he saw my secrets and hidden pain? Maybe he was trying to get me to see what he had seen? But that would mean that my dad recognized the same rage and anger in me that I had seen in him. Maybe his direct stare was him saying *you* can have this same grace and mercy and forgiveness that I have found. I could not accept the idea that he would see my pain, the hurts and secrets I had hidden away from view, it made me uncomfortable, vulnerable. By the time we arrived home I brushed it all aside.

I believe anger is a necessary emotion, it drives us past our fears to do things we may never have the courage to do; it pushes us past our co-dependencies, but when anger turns to rage it shuts us down and stops us dead in our tracks. Even in the darkest of rages there is grace and mercy that can guide all of us to forgive ourselves. To forgive ourselves is to love ourselves and to love ourselves is to love God. That's what my dad gave me in those moments; in his laugh... it was the example of the first layer of forgiveness; to forgive one's self.

I would visit my father only two more times after seeing him changed. The very last time I saw him I was in Erie at a build site working with Habitat for Humanity. We were building a home for a gentleman who worked several jobs trying to make ends meet for his family of five children and his wife, he was studying to be an anesthesiologist, while working at a local nursing facility. We had the opportunity to meet at the build site because Habitat requires the recipients of the home to work a required number of hours on their own homes and the homes of others. In talking with him he stated that I looked so familiar to him, he felt like we had met before. I explained that my father was in a facility not far from the site. He was shocked by this and looked at me strangely, as if a light came on, he smiled, tilted his head and said,

"You're one of Johnny's girls, wow I thought you looked familiar; I see your face every day on his wall."

I looked at him curiously as he explained that he worked with my father every day at the nursing facility and stated that my picture hung on his corkboard next to his bed. I looked at him suspiciously and then said how funny it was that we should meet like this, and he stopped what he was doing and looked directly at me.

"No, that's God," he said.

I was building a home with and for the man that was taking care of my dad and was expected to believe that my other father (God), just may have had something to do with that? It made me uncomfortable to think of God being a caring loving being.

Dawn Feldman-Steis

Nonetheless I went that evening to see my dad and when I walked in, he was already in bed. He lit up the same way since the day of the laugh. He never lost that light; his eyes clear and shining, happy to see me. I told him about the build and what had happened, and then before leaving I took one long look at him and somehow, I knew that it would be the last time I saw dad. He was healthy and doing well but I just knew it was our last visit. I began to cry a bit as I bent over to kiss his forehead, he looked concerned about this so I sucked up the tears and told him I loved him, and I would see him soon. What an honor it was to meet the caregiver of my father and have the opportunity to give something back to him. Looking back, the universe and the perfect timing of God never ceases to amaze me when we ponder to look at how the pieces of our lives are assembled.

The last time I saw my dad was in September of '93. I remember being bewildered by the visit but thankful for it. Early one Saturday morning in November the nursing home called. There had been an accident because Dad had attempted to get out of his chair the night before and get into bed on his own and had fallen in the process. He was being transported to a local medical center to undergo surgery for a broken hip. They would keep us posted on a status. I questioned how this could happen when he was supposed to have a lap belt on to prevent him from attempting to get up on his own. Dad would do that, try to do things for himself unwilling to accept that he didn't have the strength. He had atrophied so much with the lack of movement in his body that he was quite frail physically, though his mind was intact. My friend from habitat was not present at the time of the incident so could tell us nothing. I prayed so hard for a good outcome, even though I hadn't really been a prayer before. But I prayed on that day, and I waited and prayed and waited and waited. Finally, the phone rang, and it was my grandmother: everything went well, the hip was repaired, and all looked good. I was relieved; my stepdad, God, had really been there, looking out for my biological, dad and maybe this prayer thing works?

Or maybe not. The next morning, on November 16th, another call came in from the hospital informing us that although the surgery went well it seemed that there were complications, bone fragments undetected during surgery had punctured my dad's lung, and there was slow bleeding into his lung. They could not operate as they felt he could not survive another surgery; they would attempt to get the bleeding stopped through meds. My mother came with the news. I just sat there in my favorite highbacked chair staring out the living room window and remembered thinking about the last time I saw him, and how I felt then, that I was not going to see him again, and now knowing that I was right. I prayed but knew it was pointless. Within the hour another call came in as we were trying to arrange getting family members on the same page and driving to him, the nurse informed us that he was gone. My dad was dead, and I was lost again, and most definitely pissed off.

I drugged a lot the next few months but, even in that fog, I do remember my dad's funeral. I met with family and friends I didn't know and hugged and sat with those I did know. Funerals are funny because you never know who is going to show up. It was a nice service at the funeral home, followed by a procession to the gravesite and small service upon burial. I remember fussing over dad those couple days, seeing him in a suit for the first time and thinking how handsome he looked. Making sure things were just so. The service came and at the end, in the chapel, the family was given the opportunity to say final goodbyes and blessings before closing the casket. When my turn came, I knelt and tilted my head as I looked at him. I began to cry uncontrollably, sobbing so loud so hard. I was so mad, like Sally Fields in *Steel Magnolias*, I could not stop. I cried because of the years lost to bad choices and the stupid choices. I cried because I learned to love him and watched his soul heal and was given time to truly meet him and forgive him only to see him have to go. I cried because I was so pissed at the sick twisted son of a bitch father (God) I was left with, the one that answers prayers only to stuff them down your throat. I cried because I was uncertain what to do with the time I was left with not having to care for him. Eventually some friends walked me outdoors to get it together, to try and catch my breath. But I cried myself right back into anger again. By the time we made it to the gravesite I was solid again full of rage and cold. I buried both my dads in that dark hole that day. I put God in that hole with my father and I left him there. I was on my own and I was going to find a belief worth believing in. No more church, no more prayer, no more faith, enough with it all. And yet, the more I made choices to walk alone, the more co-dependent my life became. Perhaps my fathers, both in heaven, had a different plan for me. Isn't it funny how we begin to learn co-dependence from birth? Our parents teach us according to how they wanted to be taught, they parent how they wanted to be parented, they love how they wanted to be loved. This happened because they were not asked by their parents. It is a generational curse not to get to know our children by assuming we know best for them based on our wants and likes. We minimize the capacity of our kids trying to gain something for ourselves that we can never gain in this manner. Our parents' poor decisions become our best excuses in our own bad choices. Stepping into independence is not dictating to what we want but what, perhaps, we need to feel educated, parented and loved. What does it mean to be loved in one's own eyes, and what makes us feel heard and drives us to want to learn more? Asking questions about ourselves causes us to step away from what we have been taught and allows us to move forward into what we want to be taught… the question encourages our self-identification and defining ourselves only leads to redefining ourselves and is growth without dependence on anything. It is the start of learning to forgive ourselves because it opens us up to see the truth of what and who we are. This is the understanding and the gift that dad gave me through the years I got to know him. The idea of asking to be loved in the manner that I feel love and to forgive myself. But be warned it is not so easy and takes a step-in courage to look into our own eyes deeply and define exactly who we are in that moment. It will eventually lead us to a place where labels do not exist and one day you wake up and you take a look in that mirror and simply say...I AM.

Dawn's Angel

"The Lord God is my strength, and he will make my feet like hinds' feet, and he will make me walk upon high places." Habakkuk 3:19

So, a priest walks into a bar, no, seriously a priest walked into the bar. In 1993 I owned a bar with a partner named Denny. Denny ended up being one of the closest things to a father figure I ever had. He was a big dude, 6'5" and round. He went to school with my mother and was my first boss when I was sixteen at another local bar that would eventually burn down... Denny named the place Big Guys, one side a bar and lounge and the other side a nice little diner. Back in the earlier years of this place it was known as "The Lucky Strike". I cooked for most of the day and then closed the bar at nights. It was a Sunday evening in November of '94, in fact I am sure it was the 15th of November, about ten minutes before eight. I remember this date as it marked a year since my dad died. t was slow, we always put together a buffet on Sundays, it gave us all a bit of a break on preparing the full menu and we never had a dish boy on Sundays, everyone hates doing dishes. I let the server go early, she stated that there was one person that just came in and wanted tea. I told her to go and I would clean up and give him his tea. I went in to tear down the buffet. When I looked over, I saw this very, very skinny man writing in a small book and on a napkin. I remember thinking to myself, that he looked like he was on drugs or something. He was very thin, was wearing a well-worn flannel shirt and jeans that seemed to need a few rounds in the washer, though he himself appeared clean. (Keep in mind at this point I was fully into my routine of use... I would wake up eating speed coupled with caffeine pills and a few lines from regulars at the bar left as tips. I would speed all day and come closing time we would all find some way or another to dope. What goes up must come down. I remember thinking I had bettered myself as to the drugs I was using, compared to inhaling gasoline and paint thinner, when we were kids at the teen dances. Anyhow, maybe it takes one to know one. Looking at this guy, his skinny appearance made me recognize my 86lb frame, even more than normal, and I immediately felt uncomfortable. Thinking back on it now, everything about this guy made me uncomfortable with myself. Anyway, I walked over to the table, telling myself keep the conversation at a minimum; that maybe he would leave quickly if I didn't engage him. I asked if he needed anything. I asked what he was doing all that writing for? He looked up at me and there was no addiction in this man's eyes, just unwavering conviction. I found him, in that moment, scary and disturbing. He told me he was a priest from Ontario Canada, and that he had been traveling for the past few months trying to find a new location for a church in the states. He explained that he had run short of money and was returning to Canada to regroup and ask God what's next. During this conversation I was arrogantly looking the other way acting uninterested all the while sitting down in the chair across from him. (In my head I was screaming, what are you doing Dawn!?) It was so automatic to just sit down and yet the last thing I wanted to do. I explained that I was going to close up soon and the food would be tossed out, he was welcome to grab a plate and help himself on the house. I couldn't figure out why I was drawn to this man, why I had sat down, why I was suddenly willing to prolong my day, especially as I promised that I would never help another Christian again. (My thinking then was that most Christians find themselves in these messes because they give too much and act like they will save the world on nothing, because they gave it all away.) This was all followed up by my pride that I would bail out this holy man with a free meal, when clearly, he had issues with his own church. Justified by my kindness, I went back to cleaning up. I remember his intimidating stare being not as bothersome after a while.

Two plates of food and three cups of tea later and it was getting late. We had some brief conversations, mainly small talk, as I went back and forth between the kitchen and the dining area. He began to shuffle through his pockets searching for a tip and finally, he stood up. He was very tall, this man, over six feet by some inches. The shadows in the dimly lit room made him appear even taller. I followed him to the door quietly hoping not to encourage small talk. Once he was gone, I would lock up, then transfer registers in the bar and hang with the regulars and relax. I was agitated and ready to sit with the misery I called company, but this fellow moved slow. Then, just when I thought I was free and clear, this guy turns and asks if he can pray for me. (We don't know how very powerful that sentence is until we truly find our knees.) I felt my face turn red. I was so angry, and my reasoning kicked in and I thought to myself he won't leave until you say sure. No problem right it's a prayer, he'll feel better. I thought to myself no big deal just let him pray go through the motion and he will leave. But this guy was an odd one; this guy did not bow his head, he did not reach for my hand, or put his hand on my shoulder, oh no. This man bent down on both knees and grabbed both my feet as if he were holding on for his own life. His grip was tight and strong, and he began to pray for... wait for it... my shoes! That's right, this dude felt it necessary to pray for my boots that they lead me down the path of Blah Blah, and keep me protected as a guide until something. I don't recall all he said. I was in total shock that any of this was happening. It was one of those moments when you look away and talk to yourself as if looking in a mirror and say why? Why am I letting this happen, screaming in my own head, this is so AWKWARD? I realize now that what was so awkward just may have been the most humbling act I have ever witnessed. He stood up thanked me, walked out the door, and I locked it all while my mouth was still hanging wide open. I stood there staring for bit thinking to myself, what just happened? I was more shaken by my own actions then his and he was acting very strange for sure.

I walked through the small hallway that leads to the bar and my regulars asked where I had been and what took so long. I remember I jeered and said my last customer just prayed on my boots! Can you imagine that, my boots! They all busted out laughing. See I had just bought these new boots, fresh out on the market. I had been telling folks that Sketchers were up and coming, the new best thing, and they all thought my boots were the ugliest thing ever. They had been busting on me for days. So of course when I said someone had prayed over them you can imagine the jokes. Someone mumbled, "They needed prayer, but those shoes are still ugly", or "you can't pray the ugly off them". They were all convinced that sketchers would never catch on. And if most of them weren't dead I would probably go back and rub that in a bit now.

The next day, when I arrived at work, I found the napkin he'd written on, the typical John 3:16 God is gonna save you. He signed it and said, "THANK YOU FOR ALLOWING ME TO PRAY WITH YOU!" I was shocked. I was pissed really, how would he know that, before he left the table, before he asked me to pray, that I would agree to pray with him? That night changed me, not profoundly, not in some outrageous "I found the missing GOD kind of way". It was little things; I unconsciously started using less, remarkably enough that friends noticed. My friend Annie would be the first; she sat next to me some time during the next week and ask me what's wrong Stoner? You aren't partying with us? It was slight small thoughts. Simple reflections of my own cruelty would come to mind. My partying days were numbered, and it was because I allowed for a moment a slight crack in my anger and hate to let a prayer touch me. I said sure let's pray. And now I wanted to know why. I felt stalked and hungry all at the same time. I could see things a bit differently. It was slight, but things had changed. All my fears would haunt me at once and I could not wrestle with the anxiety and be high or doped up… What used to numb those fears now made them worse. By the end of the month I would be in full blown detox/withdrawal, and at the end of six months I would be completely clean of any drug including aspirin. Coming out of that shit I found myself at 79 lbs., my skin was tight and stretched over my face. My tongue was split from the tip to the back of my throat from dehydration. I had a urinary tract infection so severe that the lymph nodes in my groin were swollen the size of golf balls. The muscle cramps just to come down the stairs would set me to tears, tears that would break my spirit and crush my pride. I would visit the doctor for the first time, and he would gasp at the sight of me, but he dug in and with the strongest voice said we will do this, you will make it. I would run fevers so high I wished to die. I would come to know the passions of a best friend (my ex-husband) and a mother to help me to stand up and get back to it. It would be 14 years before I would pray again. But I really believe that every day that passed from that initial night until I would bow down in prayer again that many people kept me lifted in prayer and presented to God as valuable. Whether I knew it or I not, I was held, I was worthy.

The whole experience poises a question deep inside that if I dare, I already know the answer to. Johns' Angel? You know the guy that told him all about himself and told him to quit drinking and live a life better: Could that stranger sitting next to my dad in the bar seven years ago be the same stranger to grab hold of my feet and pray in a dimly lit dining room late on a lazy Sunday night? Could it possibly be our angel, or maybe John sent him knowing I needed to have at least a presence of change and protection from something higher than my own thinking. Whatever the reason, there was no coincidence to it.

And the boots?! Those damn boots have lasted all this time and continue to carry me, they are a bit worn and look like they've been through it, but they fit just right, and I don't think I could ever replace them. They have been through flood waters and fires. Hiking with friends, kayaking, they have had tears on them and scrapes along the way. They have wrestled with anger and waged wars. They have stood in protest lines and chased after a young child only to see him to manhood. They have become a tangible reflection of God in my life, to an angel least noticed and most needed. But where I once thought they would lead me, I'm realizing, all these years later, that I directed them on my path. They have taught me that we all have this nobility inside of us, that it's deeply innate, and when we learn to bend down, humble ourselves, and pray for someone's boots, we find it. When we step courageously into someone's life and tell them to change and to see differently, we find it. It's in this nobility that we find God; it strips us of pride and eliminates the co-dependency of this world. We spend our lives trying to understand the nobility of God. As we learn faith, trust, love, and hope we accept this place in God's kingdom, we learn to take a knee or two and pray for our neighbors, our friends and our lost. I would say twenty-eight years out from addiction, what I know, what I have learned, is freedom. I can tell you I am now free of fear, hate, and drugs, but also free to love, trust, and hold others, and to appreciate every day as a chance to embrace all of this life in all of its labels and find that the true definition to a life well lived is to have no definition at all.

The Wages of
Sin is Death

"Applied Knowledge almost always implies change"

The scriptures and ancient texts have many things to say about sin. Most of these passages insight or aim to insight a fear based on a life ending in hell or burning fire away from a reward in heaven. Some beliefs are more restrictive than others. I spent so many years wandering in fear and hanging on the faith of others that it wasn't until later in life that I looked at sin and the many meanings it holds for folks.

The Bible itself has an array of sins and the answer to most of them is Mercy and Forgiveness. I have been shown God's mercy so many times, in so many ways. It's almost difficult to pick through the stories to bring the point at hand forward. As an intro I will say that we see sin prior to Moses as different as there really weren't any rules established until Moses. But God does remove Adam and Eve from the garden after disobeying and Cain after killing his brother, is marked and cursed to be apart, from not only God but from his family. In the book of Enoch, it is explained, that Able cries out to continuously, as he waits to be reunited with God but cannot until God sends his son to die for the sins of men. Yet Able did not sin, his brother did? But what does it really mean to sin? How does God judge sin? And is it possible to truly live without sin in this skin form. In all the scriptures and holy text, if we take a look at the sinners that God punished, those sins are not what we today would consider the bad sins, or even the worst sins. They were separated from God because they ate a fruit and disobeyed, cursed because of murder, stripped because of pride. And always the punishment for the sin is separation from God both in our spirits and physically.

I remember when God was first starting to move me back toward a study with him instead of about him. I had decided earlier in my life to study other holy texts and as many other beliefs as I possibly could fit in my head. I had had a talk with God and explained that I needed to step away for a bit. I needed to know a life without a God in order to better understand a life with a God. I had recently been reading a book by William Henry called *The Cloak of the Illuminati,* and had been practicing aligning my chakras and energies for self-healing. Through all this learning I began to see that all beliefs led to the same God head. That they were all fragments of a whole, not to be judged but to be acquired and applied, for the purpose of being closer to God. God can use just about anything to shock us back into reality and into our purpose.

In my case it was December 30, 2006, a Saturday morning. I woke up early and picked up something to look at or read through, grabbed a cup of coffee and curled up on the sofa. My son was off with his father for the weekend and I always enjoyed a quiet Saturday morning when he was away. I grabbed the remote to look at a bit of news. The very first thing I saw was a man with a black bag over his head, rope already tightened around his neck, one minute he was standing there and the next just hanging dead. I was like, WTF is this? And Who and Why is this on TV. The next thing I saw was a news flash, and the camera panning to nations all over the world with folks standing in the street celebrating. People were jumping up and down, yelling and chanting. Bewildered I decided it best to turn up the volume and find out what was going on. So, I turned it up, switched to a different channel and watched again. What I was witnessing that Saturday morning wasn't a ritual cartoon or daily informative TV program but the fulfillment of

Saddam Hussein's death sentence. In the second viewing they showed pictures of a broken, run-down man that knew nothing of power anymore. I remember when they pulled Saddam out of his hiding hole and thinking to myself, wow, he looks old and tired. He looks like the life he has lived, the hell he has brought to so many has been drawn through the lines on his face, his eyes so dark and cold. I watched as he walked toward the steps with no struggle in him and climbed up to the platform. There was some discussion of what would be happening next from the men accompanying him and then a bag was placed over his head, then the rope and the boards dropped, and it was over.

In that moment I was broken. I sat there in shock of what I witnessed and began to cry, not just a tear but a full-on sloppy wailing sob. I gathered myself, sipped some coffee and wondered what the hell was wrong with me. I was not usually big on tears and was most definitely not someone who sobbed at random. I thought Jesus?!, this guy had it coming, what is wrong with me? I was clearly having some sort of psychological breakdown. I began to wonder if there is a gas leak in the house or maybe something in the coffee. But it would not stop. I cried most of the day, mumbling all the while as to why this would ever bother me. I briefly paused and took note that maybe I wasn't seeing the same reality that my spirit was witnessing. So, I sat back down, and I got quiet and still, and I said simply, God? After six years of not praying once and not really taking notice of a God presence around me, I asked again.

"God? If there is something I should see or learn through this? Show me clearly. God, I know I have asked that you step away, but I need you to show me where you are in this mess. I can't seem to see this clearly and I would like to see your presence regarding current events. I mean really God where do you stand with this man dying and nations of people rejoicing in his death. It seems so barbaric and to stoop to his level to watch nations celebrate murder. Justified or not? I mean really, an eye for an eye, right? But it feels so wrong."

I went about my busy work and every time I heard it or watched it again, I would break all over again. Closer towards evening I thought to myself he was someone's grandpa, he was someone's husband, brother, he was someone's baby and at some point, he knew love and connection and those connections are now watching him die over and over again. Saddam did not have the best life. He had terrible parents and was raised by an asshole uncle, but at some point, he knew love. How awful we can be in our human forms and how we feel justified to be so awful.

I went to sleep that night still broken, still heavy, still mourning. I dreamt of being hung myself that night. I dreamt of being electrocuted and gassed that night. Every time I woke up, I would just go back to sleep to a different demise. By the next day I had not slept and realized I had not eaten, and I wasn't hungry, and I had no desire to try and rest more. I thought I would just ignore the events of yesterday, push it out of my mind and stay busy. Surely this will go away, still trying to justify through Knowledge of his crimes that he deserved to die. Every time you picked up a newspaper or magazine or turned on the TV or radio you had to hear that story all over again. Then God spoke and showed me an ever-changing picture of those events. Every time I watched, it changed. I went to bed the second night and I had a dream about Saddam as a man of great power using it in all the wrong ways, then Saddam as a young man looking for direction, all the way back to Saddam in the womb. But the dream took me even farther back. I was standing in a position to look over a woman's shoulder. As I looked over, this women's hands were cupped together holding a very tiny very bright child. She breathed on this child and said I am giving you to the world and your name will be Saddam and you will do GREAT things! I woke that morning in tears again with a different understanding and a different sight. I watched the taping of his death once more. This time as I watched him walking toward the platform, I witnessed a humbled man, moving calmly but not alone. I witnessed a broken man climbing the steps not in fear but in the understanding that this was a new beginning for him. I realized as I witnessed his death that he had to die for his crimes as the world/law dictates, but what I saw with all of my being, beyond any knowledge, was God standing right by his side and when he was hung. God hung with him. But here was the true mind blower... The men in the room with him, the men doing the hanging... God was present with them also. God was standing next to every person around the world that celebrated Saddam's death. He was present always, everywhere no matter the crime, no matter the personal belief, no matter the knowledge. God was just present. God was not out floating here and there he was not sitting on a cloud or creating a new world for only good people, he was not a tiny Jesus sitting on a throne in my heart, he was with me every minute, always in his/her I AM way (the I AM is a whole different story for later). He was present when Saddam took his first life in murder and he was present when Saddam took his last breath. Saddam knew grace and forgiveness and no matter how much our minds want to believe that he is burning in hell, it just isn't so. Whether he met Jesus face to face in his hiding hole or he repented during his walk to death. God picked up his soul, cupped it in his hands and said Saddam you did GREAT things, great terrible things, but I love you. I created you, you will not walk alone. This is the God we are asked to believe in. An all-forgiving God of love, grace, and mercy, and to see God's presence we must at least believe that his forgiveness is for all of us. That's the rub with God. No matter our judgments of right and wrong God choses love and forgiveness. I needed to sit back and ponder this for a bit of time. It took a while to digest it, because if I was going to continue to believe in an all-forgiving, all-loving God,

I had to buy in to the fact that all people were worthy of God's grace and mercy— murderous tyrants and compassionate leaders alike.

*

We so long to put a face to sin, as if we will be better able to recognize it if sin has a face. If we can make sin a picture, then maybe it won't be so easy to sin. We also like to place levels to the sin in the world. You know, the bank robber that kills his hostages is much worse than Johnny who stole a loaf of bread to feed his family. But you see, what I witnessed and came to know very personally that weekend is that both love and evil are actions, and that God has no level to any of them. In God's eyes sin is sin and love is love. Period. Simple as that. No matter what you have done, where you have been; dictator of a nation or bully in high school you are worthy of God's forgiveness. I was given a gift to be witness of that which few choose to understand. There are simple truths that we are shown, pillars, that are ineffable, that once learned stay with us always. They are so revealed into the fibers of our spirits that it's hard to even explain the truth that's been shown. The fact remains that there is no level to sin in God's eyes, to sin is simply to separate yourself from God and to separate yourself from God is death to the spirit he created in you. To specify sin in levels creates our first connection to co-dependence within our capacity of belief.

Something happened to my thinking in those three days, not my knowledge but in the deepest core of my being. Maybe it was a seed planted, or a scar removed. Whatever it was I know this. It was painful and freeing, passionate and redemptive and I will never be the same. I witnessed firsthand the excruciating love and presence of God, not through a sermon or a simple faith, But through the possibility of redemption and forgiveness of a once ruthless dictator. Saddam did do great things, great horrible things, but in his final act of life he was a witness of God's presence, even

Dawn Feldman-Steis

if the witness was only witnessed by myself. Knowing that God speaks to each of us at the time of our creation and breathes life into our souls with the declaration of YOU WILL DO GREAT THINGS is a game changer. We have all done great things, great terrible things and great miracles. Whether our hand is causing damage or building up new, he is present. He dies with the murders and is born every day with our children. I have never known the full power of that weekend in the same way since, but every now and again I catch a line in a hymn or hear a story from a friend and I am reminded of Saddam. A tossed away child, raised by and asshole uncle, determined and driven, a man who lost his way to power and ego. And in his evil actions he was still worthy of love and forgiveness. That's the promise of God, forgiveness of all sins without the limitations of sin in levels.

That's what we have done as Christians, what I have railed against most of life not truly understanding my rebellion. I have come know that what I wanted to find was that independent place with God, that connection that didn't require a church or congregation, it didn't require a specific prayer or the need to speak a tongue for interpretation. The realization that the God we believe in forgives and loves without limitation, and that it is us who form a co-dependence with God, creating unhealthy relationships with our own innate beliefs all because it's easier to think that the bad guy is unforgivable and goes to hell and the good guy lives eternally. So, there it is the beginning of my free and independent belief in a God that is capable of anything. There it is me starting to understand a deeper connection to creation and my belonging to it.

I remember sharing this story for the first time with a longtime family friend and mentor. I had grown up going to bible studies and prayer meetings in her home during the Eighties; we never missed a Wednesday night and most times I found myself hiding or sleeping under the coffee table. I shared my new findings and understanding, so excited that I could actually buy into this concept of an all-loving God, with all the confidence that she would embrace my truth and completely understand my new insights. Yea, the homecoming I was expecting, well that didn't happen. Oh, she did not agree at all. She explained that some people have done things so bad and are so far gone that they just can't be forgiven and went on to explain that Saddam wasn't even a Christian and did not believe in God, at least not our God. She continued to say how we need to surrender all these thoughts and thinking and really get into the word and determine what God wants of us. I knew in this very moment two things: One, that what God had shown me about grace and mercy was not going anywhere and the joy from the knowing was going to stay with me forever, not even a lifelong mentor could steal it away, and Two, that I was clearly embarking on a journey that was my own and I couldn't take anyone with me. It was mine to travel.

What I knew about Saddam, that this mentor didn't, was that Saddam fancied himself to be the reincarnation of King Nebuchadnezzar. I find that interesting, simply because king Nebuchadnezzar was the first gentile king really mentioned in the bible, and though it took him several visions and signs he still was proud and boastful of himself, it wasn't until his final days that he truly testified to the forgiveness and mercy of God. He had to be stripped of his titles and was made to crawl through the fields like the oxen and he was made to eat grass for seven years, because of pride. He had murdered and stolen lands and fought wars and attempted to kill Gods chosen, and God found his pride to be so much more offensive than all that, that he stripped him of his titles and made him eat grass. He was humbled and forgiven, and I can't help but to think and to know that the same happened for Saddam.

I am sure at this point that I have concerned some readers and some of you may even be pissed off, and that's ok. It's hard to hear that God loves a person like Saddam, it's hard to acknowledge that

Dawn Feldman-Steis

our beliefs in God's grace and mercy extend even to our greatest enemies, and many of us may not truly know the extent of God's love in our lifetimes, but those of us that do, have a responsibility to try and share it to the best of our ability. That is what I want to do, is try and explain and show how God has revealed the ultimate love for us.

My favorite bible guy is Enoch, not because he never knew death or that he was like a favorite pet student, but because he mustered every bit of courage he had, stood up as tall as he could, and he went to God and petitioned/interceded for Gods own Angels. Think about that, a simple human standing before God in the strongest prayers requesting mercy for Gods very own Angels. It takes a bit of courage to petition for a friend or relative, it takes much more courage to petition for an enemy, but to intercede for the congregations of heaven well, that shit's noble. That is, as I have said before, what we all strive for is Enoch's nobility. To get to a place where we can intercede not just for our enemies but for the congregations of the heavens.

Our thoughts of sins, and the layers of them keep us dependent on the church and further separate us from an independent belief in God—it hushes the divine with in us. We cannot live without sin, we all know this, but we can recognize those things in our lives that personally create a separation between ourselves and our creator. That's the push when it comes to sin, determining the right course individually and intimately with in our beliefs, and living graciously and mercifully in the presence of an omnipotent, omnipresent God. It takes faith and belief to have that courage.

I am a tyrant and a bully; I am forgiveness and mercy. What if we look at the tyrant and bully and notice the co-dependence in their actions, are also in our actions? What if forgiveness and mercy and our ability to accept them comes from our capacity to correct the tyrant and bully in ourselves?

Eight Hours to Fairmont

"Those who don't believe in magic will never find it."
—Roald Dahl

I had a dream sometime in the spring of 2007. I had been doing some research into a few different belief systems as well as my family ancestry. Between understanding auras better and figuring out what this Voodoo was all about, I began to question the truths found in all of it and realized that there was this connectivity that drives us toward being independent in our beliefs. Almost all of us have these experiences in our lives, only a few write them down, others share them, and others keep them close, but they are there just the same, and they carry the same lessons and open us to similar truths unique to us finding them. I had been dreaming almost every night about crazy things due to the course and focus of study. Dreams are funny, sometimes they are what we ate before bed or watched on TV. Sometimes they are brought on by heartbreak or trauma, and sometimes they come from nowhere and seem to transport us to places we might not ever have known unless we took the courage during our walks in the astral plains to dare and step forward.

In the dream I was standing at the top of a driveway that dipped down into a small valley. At the bottom was a bridge that crossed over a small creek, and as you crossed to the other side on the hill, there stood a large farmhouse. The house, as expected, was a historic whitewashed farmhouse in the middle of the field at the edge of the forest. I stood watching the area for a bit. There was no movement, no breeze or birds flying; but the colors of everything was so vivid and bright. I began to walk down the driveway. I could hear and feel the gravel give way to each step as I moved down the small hill and across the wooden bridge. I noticed the red door to the farmhouse was open and inviting. I walked up to the door and pushed it further open to step into the family room. To my left was another small room with a tiny table, with an oil lamp and a wooden box on top. There was one high backed armchair just next to the tiny table. The lamp told me we had traveled backward for the moment and the chair told me that they had more than enough for comfort. In front of me was a wide doorway. Clearly this was a dining room with an old farm table where eight to ten chairs could fit. Around this table a group of men stood. The lighting was dim. I don't recall any windows now that I think on it. I walked forward into the dining room and I could feel the men's recognition to my presence. One gentleman looked directly at me as to say I see you; I know you're there, but I was just a witness to the events taking place, in the room but not part of it. I worked my way into the group and looked onto the table and there lay a woman, in a long brown linen shirt with brown linen short pants no socks and a pair of untied lace up black leather shoes. They had placed salt around the bottom of her feet, but not her whole body, they have sewn her mouth shut and possibly her eyes. As I walked the side of the table up toward her head, I recognized her looking at me, also as if to say you are a witness here. I walked around the top of the table and down the other side all the while the gentlemen short in height and stern in his look watched me, he had glasses and lighter colored hair combed over and parted on the side, as if he was keeping tally of something. From here I would leave the circle of people and veer off the line into the kitchen to find all the women siting and cooking. They would speak of her and her passing not negatively but more out of relief that they would not have to endure her medicines and remedies any longer. I got a sense of real stronghold of energy surrounding the whole event, and as I began to go toward the door to leave, I felt and heard the sound of rushing footsteps behind me coming faster and faster until the loudness of it woke me up. The dream left an impression. Not for any particular detail but just thinking about it I could hear the rushing of the footsteps again and the sense of someone behind me. In my sixth sense I felt it to be past family that I had spent time with on a separate plain.

As I talked with family and friends about the dream that day, I could hear the rushing again, as if the group of angry ancestors were coming to prevent me to speak of it. To try and stop me here in this time from the past. Every time I spoke of the funeral or death, I would feel her close. I had two more dreams of this woman, that at some point I started to call Ruth, though she never gave her name. In one of them I helped her to cut the strings from her mouth, I looked at her and said who are you? She simply said, "I am you 150 years removed." Then she walked away, and I have not dreamed of her since. I do feel her presence here and there and most definitely call her attention when I speak about her. But what did she mean when she said I am you 150 years removed? I pondered it over and over, I knew she was family, family from generations ago but had no idea what to do about it. I decided out of nowhere really, I was going to West Virginia and find this house and would find all the answers when I did. I just suddenly knew that I knew where it was, and I was going to accomplish whatever it was I was to do with all this dream had shown me. Or at least get some answers. Like if I put my feet on the ground all the ghosts of the generations before would appear before me and tell me what was needed. Right?

So of course, when we have such a dream, we talk about them. I first told my mother and then I told her that I as heading to West Virginia the next weekend to look around. She said without a

moment's hesitation, 'I will be there Friday, and I will go with you.'"
My mother never does the spur of the moment thing. Being the true
libra that she is everything takes planning and rehearsing and most
definitely balance. It caught me as funny as I was hanging up that
evening, but it would be good to spend the time. I went into work
that next morning and again found myself talking about the dream
to friends there. One of my closest friends (she's a bestie) worked
with me at the time. Our offices consisted of several large rooms
with cubical walls in them to maximize the amount of service
coordinators that we could fit into one office, the business was
growing and so each office had four or more people in it depending
on the size of the room. My friend Cimone and another colleague
that I became friends with, Emeril, both sat in the same office
together. I walked in with my coffee and started to tell them about
this crazy dream, after I was done, I proudly announced that I
would be going to West Virginia come the weekend and threw
in that when I told my mother about it, she automatically said
she would be down Friday. No sooner was this said and Cimone
said I am going and then Emily said I am going! And just like the
fellowship of the dream was formed and we were all heading to
West Virginia, and no one really knew why? I did not ask them to
go they just said they were going and that was that.

Saturday morning was finally here, and we were going on a
journey, yay, I love a journey. My mom had made cheese sandwiches
as was the tradition in my family when embarking on trips to West
Virginia. During family vacations the car would be packed to
the gills with suitcases for five people and a big old sack lunch of
cheese spread sandwiches, chips and cokes for all. In keeping with
the tradition Penny made sandwiches and had them at the ready.
Cimone came to the house and we were set to pick up Emeril on our
way. Let me explain our posse for a moment only because it does
matter in this moment. Penny is a bible carrying long time Christian

women ready to take on the demons of the generational curses that may pose any threat toward me or anyone with us, she is armed and at the ready. Emeril was our youngest member but wise beyond her years, she was/is a pagan and came toting her pendulum and spiritual sight, she is armed and at the ready. We put the warriors in the back seat together. That's funny now. Cimone and I at the time had deep foundations of belief and understanding, we had faith, but we weren't talking about it. We had both been away from identifying spiritually but both had clearly defined understandings. One other thing about Cimone, she is black, and she was heading straight into the Appalachian Mountains, I am sure she may have said a few prayers of safety for herself and the group, trust and believe she was armed and at the ready. Myself? Well, I had bright white, blonde short spikey hair still a bit angry with the Christian muck of my childhood and excited to find new beliefs to roll them up into one big mess, caught up in a world of labels and proud to throw those labels at folks as to measure the shock and awe that I got back from those listening. Two of us identified as bisexual and one of us identified as lesbian, and my mom identified as straight, but she loved us all anyway. LOL. We were a car full of labels and stereotypes and we were heading to Fairmont, WV.

When they said chase those dreams, I don't think they meant this. It was about a three-hour drive to Mannington/Fairmont, WV from Silver Spring, MD. Being who I am I decided, without the advice from others, that we could scoot through the mountains the back way. It would take a bit longer but give us some time to hang and enjoy the ride, the Shenandoah river valley is fantastically beautiful. I had it all mapped out, in my head. We drove and drove... and stopped and asked where we were and then drove some more. About five hours in, my mother suggested that we find a hotel and a six pack of beer and call it a day; and Emeril agreed. Our warriors were getting wary. We drove into Maryland, then West Virginia, then back to Virginia and back into West Virginia. We were going in circles and could not figure out the next turn, and who brought a map? No one. Cell phones were not as handy as they are today. Finally, on a very winding mountain road Penny suggested we pull over when we found a place to do so. So, I did and Cimone pointed to a biker bar and suggested we go there but that Penny should go first, that they were her people. My mother was born and raised and lived a good bit of her young life in West Virginia, and we spent many summers in the mountains with Great Grandma. We were not the sort of group that was seen in these here parts on a regular basis though. Anyhow we walked into the dinning area and everything stopped and got as quiet as quiet could get, so quiet we also stopped, and everyone just stared at each other. After a long moment of silence and assessment, Penny energetically moved toward the waitress, explaining that we were lost. As soon as those words came out of her mouth the room went back into motion… so funny looking back on it. The waitress did not even know where Fairmont was, but some customers did, and they explained that if we just stayed north on the road, we would find it. Back in the car, and on the road, we went, and we drove and drove. It did not help matters that we had to slow down in some places as the road narrowed and there was no guard rail protecting us from the 100 foot drop off on the side of the mountain. Heads were shaking, folks began complaining and comments such as "let's just turn around" started coming from the back seat. Then something stirred in my friend Cimone, something got up under her skin and she started declaring and in a stern voice, with her hands now holding onto the "oh shit bar" attached to the dash, she said "We are going to Fairmont." Above our voices and complaints she continued: "Oh we are fucking going to Fairmont."

We all looked at her she smacked her lips and said it again even louder: "I said we are fucking going to Fairmont; do you hear me? We are not stopping until we get to Fairmont."

She continued to declare and yell at the would-be invisible force preventing us from finding our way. About two and a half hours later, after leaving the diner we made it to Fairmont. Just in time for the sun to start setting. Dusk was upon us as we drove up the small road to Begum cemetery in Mannington West Virginia.

We had just a bit of light while looking at the grave markers, Henan's and Yost's. I looked at them all hoping to find one that would stand out, that would catch me in the gut, and I could connect the women in the dream to this tangible object. Nope, that did not happen. There were brief comments on Emeril's last name, Yost, intertwined in the family cemetery. What were the odds of that happening? What were the odds of us all standing in a West Virginia cemetery on the back side of a mountain?

We spent the rest of the daylight there and as dusk settled in, we got back into the car and headed down the road. As we got to the bottom of the hill you could see my great grandmother's house off to the distance, abandoned and unloved. To the right was the house! The house I saw in the dream, the driveway did not seem as long, but it was the house just the same. Penny said, "Go on, drive down in there, go on." You could see Cimone take a deep breathe in and I was bitching about whether they would have dogs. I did not spend the last eight hours with these people complaining to end this thing by getting chewed up by a dog. A woman in her mid-forties, maybe a bit older came out of the house and met us all in the driveway. We all stayed close to the car, after all we all know what happens in West Virginia when you take a wrong turn. My mother did most of the talking. She explained that we were taking a trip down memory lane and that her grandmother lived just across the way. The woman explained that they had been attempting to build a second home on the land and had run into issue after issue with the new house. The old house being the one that was in my dream with its whitewashed stick-built frame and red roof and door. It was charming and comforting to stand in front of it like I had been there always. Penny and the woman finished talking and we all got back in the car. I sat there staring for a bit and Emily and Penny said, "you aren't done yet, are you?" You still need to be here?" I said yes. My mother then got out of the car and walked up to the door and spoke with the woman again, she explained that since we had come all this way and she had had so much trouble lately, would she mind if we prayed over her land and home?

Meanwhile Emily Cimone and I sat in the car and spoke in low voices, asking each other what we thought Penny was up there saying to that woman. Penny returned to the car and said we were good to go. I said go where and she said we could walk wherever we wanted on the property and pray and do whatever we have to do.

Now let me ask you: In what world do folks make a choice and say I am gonna follow your dream with you and then when you get to your destination and are greeted by a woman, home alone, and this woman lets you and your three companions wander onto her property, in the black of night and gives you all permission to do whatever you need to do? How does that happen?

We all got out of the car. Excitement came over us on the dirt driveway as Emily handed me a pendulum and Penny grabbed her bible from the back seat. Like I said these folks were armed and at the ready. We began to walk with nothing but fireflies and moonlight. It was dark and we were walking through a large field at the bottom of the hill in front of the house. We walked a way into the field following the movement of the pendulum and then stopped. Thank God for moonlight because it was very dark. The four of us, unintentionally, stood as the arrows of a compass. At least that's how I see it now. I stood at the east with my back to the tree line, Emily to the north with her back to the tree line, Penny to the west with her back to the house and Cimone to the south with her back to the open hill. As we stood there, we discussed how we could feel that we weren't alone. I mean, that could have been because of the dream or too many movies or maybe we really were amongst company from past lives and secrets that only the trees dared to speak of. We felt it but could see nothing. We all prayed in that field in the dark. We prayed for the owners of the land, and for the property to be safe, and we prayed that anything bound to this land was free to leave and move on. At one point I wanted to lay down. Cimone said "do it, go ahead" but Emeril said, "Don't it smells like we were standing over a septic tank or maybe we were in a septic field. Does anyone else smell that?" But what would happen if I lied down, Emily emphatically said, "but don't!"

We all watched the pendulum go from moving to still to moving again that night. We stood at opposites from each other and yet we have been connected forever in a way none of us could describe. We stood in solidarity of spirit all in separate directions. To this day I believe that if one of us called all the others at any time and said they had a dream or had a leading, without any hesitation, every one of us would buckle up and jump to action and follow it. We finished up our business, walked back to the car, waved at the women as we went by and started on our way home. The car ride was quiet on the three-hour drive home, Cimone and I talked briefly about what any of this meant. Penny and Emily napped in the back seat. It was a strange feeling. I did not really know why or how we all came together, and it did not appear that we had done anything with regard to the dream or satisfying the excitement of possibly seeing one hundred- and fifty-year-old ancestors. There was this sense of bewilderment and yet complete accomplishment all at the same time and we never really said anything more about it again. We went back to life and work and back to business as usual.

In a way I think that, for whatever reason, we all needed this experience at the same time in our lives. Here are my thoughts regarding the group and becoming independent. We have all been taught the black and white of what is wrong and what is right. But there are these immense gray areas, it's within these areas that religion and its leadership dare to reach out and grasp a person's sole and manipulate it with fear. They make bold concrete statements concerning faith and belief to keep those listening stuck in place. I mean, let's face it, if you promote independence you promote an empty house of worship and if the seats are bare the collection plate is also. They will teach things like shows with magic and witchcraft are wrong and you're a sinner to watch them, or pagans are not acting in God's love. Pagan leaders have said Christians are judgmental and God is nonsense. I also found it amusing when I have heard a Catholic say they are not Christian they are catholic... Ummm, Catholic is Christian because it falls under the definition of Christian, it's just one flavor. Not to mention the very nit picking of most all our places of worship. You know cursing is wrong and sex outside of marriage is bad, drinking, reading the wrong version of your holy text is wrong and the list goes on and on. Your worst hour becomes their best-earned dollar as they manipulate your faith or fear of losing your faith to keep you coming back and to keep you donating, more importantly to keep you stuck. I know it sounds mean and angry to say these things, but I am not angry, I am over being angry. I want to fix this thing we have created within our beliefs that continues to separate and destroy our differences. I want to get rid of this thing that keeps folks bound and dependent on someone else's interpretation of faith and how to act on it. It cuts down the dreamer and raises up spiritual zombies. I believe we can change this.

I believe our trip to Fairmont proves that it can and should be changed. How many people have left their places of worship feeling stale and stagnant or have left a faith system all together because they have been isolated or shunned for that statement that set them apart and placed them as an independent thinker. I am tired of the myths and complications driving the spirit of things. Let's change it. Let's gather in groups with all our stereo types and preconceived notions and dare to realize that those labels you have placed on others are your labels too and then let's embrace them, all of them. Each one of us made a quick choice to be in attendance with our minds but we were obedient to our spirits also and it led us on a path to find a solidarity in ourselves that day, not a reliance on the labels but and acceptance of them all. This trip was not about each person bringing a portion to the whole, it was about learning that each of us are all the portions. We are the Pagan and Christian, we are the declaration and driven, we are capable of collective acceptance within beliefs and able to embrace all truths through discernment of the facts. It comes down to the spirit being limitless, it's the auto pilot connected directly to the creative source of all things, the mind always gets in the way of this.

When we are obedient to our spirits over our minds we blend, and blending is a constant state of becoming. Let's become independent together.

A Return to Church

Your Lord is best aware of what is in yourselves. If you are righteous, then lo! He was ever forgiving unto those who turn unto Him" Quran 17:25

My son was about 14 years old when he came bounding down the stairs with all the excitement, he could hold yelling, "Hey Mom?!" as he finished swinging from the banister and jumping to miss the last three steps to land into the living room staring directly at me. I swear he never walked a step until he hit 17. He spent his whole life running jumping and tumbling everywhere we went.

"Hey mom?! I was upstairs watching a show and I want to get baptized. What do you think? How do we do that." I sat there speechless with my mouth open staring at him, in my mind thinking what the hell have I done wrong as a parent? How is this happening? I came back with, "oh boy what are you watching up there?" And he quickly responded the History channel. I wonder if I was the first parent to ponder parental controls on the History channel. I explained that it wasn't something he should go do quickly and should get a better understanding to what it really means to take that step. I was never one to push any one belief system to my son, clearly with good reason, but I always said I would support him in any direction he was searching. I never really expected it to be such a ridged request as baptism. But it was always like that with Joe, I would insist on sitting in front of the TV during dinner and he would insist on eating at the table. I would push horror movies and he would sit with the blanket over his head and say I don't wanna watch this. It is hard wired into all of us to rebel I swear its so...his form of rebellion was toward the correct pictures of perfect that have been forced into our brains. Joe and I have and continue to have a pretty cool relationship, he is a pretty cool kid. But sometimes he really just stops me in my tracks with his ideas of the way things are supposed to be in his mind and more importantly how they got there? While I am trying to be cool and hip, he is seeking out places for baptism. This wasn't a fad either he was serious and he was not just going to let it go. Off to church we go.

The next year or so was filled with opportunities for Joe. We tried a synagogue and mosque, hoping for a deterrent... he went to church with my mother a few times, road motorcycles there and had fun, but said it wasn't a real church? Went with his father and stepmom and came home said church shouldn't have folding chairs? He also determined that church should not have loud band concert type music playing during service. He was not impressed with the loud show of the fundamentals. It became clear he had a definite idea of what church was to be. We went catholic and it was too boring. I asked him to describe what church was and he couldn't, he said I will know when we get there. I liked going to all the different places seeking and learning, learning and seeking... it's what I do best. All the while praying that we find this place whatever it may be soon. At one point we were just sitting, and I said, "I am not sure what to look at first." Joe shook his head and said, "maybe it doesn't exist? Maybe they don't have what I think a church should be, have we tried everything?" I said, "no there is one we have not tried. It's the church I was baptized in." He said, "do you think they have one here by our house?" I said, "oh I am sure I will look into it and we can check it out Sunday." It had been a little over a year since we first started looking. I looked on the intra webs and found that there were actually four episcopal churches in our

Dawn Feldman-Steis

area. I brought Joe in on the plan and we agreed we would be going in the next couple weeks to check out this last hope for a church.

It was a Sunday morning late in November of 2011. I never thought I would be in this position again but off to church we went. It was a small little country church, cute. As soon as we step through the door Joe looked up and around and said, "Now this is a church." And I feeling humbled by feelings of being home and instantly comfortable said, "yes, it is." We sat down toward the back as was the rule we had established when trying new churches, this provided an easy way out in the event of crazy church antics. You know the ones, serpents and such. I was overwhelmed at how much it felt like going home that Sunday and Joe felt he had found a church finally, at least a church that suited his minds eye of what church should be. No one really rushed us, but we were greeted kindly.

The service started and Joe was all eager to participate, I find that all the rote training as a child was still intact now even after being away for so long. Joe was shocked at me knowing all the prayers and layout of the service, and I have to admit I felt a little disappointed in myself that he didn't and I never taught him, not even the lords prayer. But his belief in God is his own and he must learn to walk his path not mine. The Vicar of the church was a small, short woman from New England area, she got so excited during communion you would think she would float up off the ground, I swear she grew up there, or maybe there was a step stool...lol It was refreshing to witness all the work of the 80's had paid off in the church.

We left after service that week without attending coffee hour. Joe had started a new job and he had to get to it. The timing of this job and his want to get baptized did not go hand in hand. He was working on Weekends at the local pizza place and it seemed his schedule blocked him from church most Sundays. So, while he couldn't attend, I mysteriously could not sit home and I found myself back to church every week. The second Sunday I attended I was asked to go to coffee hour by an older gentlemen who sat behind me. Before service he had introduced himself and asked what brought me into church today, I said I had been away from organized religion for a long time, he said we won't hold that against you, many folks come that don't believe in God. I quipped back quickly with "I believe in God I don't believe in people thinking they are God." Looking back on things now I missed two very important things. That folks were in the church not to worship or believe and my belief in God was about to be tested in ways I never thought I would question. After service he tapped me on the shoulder and said come have coffee. So, I walked with him down to coffee hour and we talked a bit. The Vicar then came and sat with us for a bit, she introduced herself and we discussed a bit about why I was at the church and Joes interest in becoming baptized. She took it as seriously as I felt it was and agreed that he needed to be comfortable with the church and the Vicar to proceed not to mention the commitment he would be making. I explained his work schedule and they would meet as soon as it was possible. God is present always; work ethic is only taught in a short window in youth. I explained that I was not too comfortable with my son just jumping into a baptismal covenant with just any church and that I would continue to attend weekly. She let me know that she would be starting a bible study after the Holidays that I might like to attend, and we left it that.

I continued to attend week after week with no real reason or drive behind it. I just felt at peace in this new place and this new experience. I had experienced church as a child, and it was much different to have this time as an adult. I had a sense of control over what I took from church now and that allowed me to be free to learn what I needed and discard the rest. I noticed after a few weeks of going that I was in a place that I did not have to define myself

Dawn Feldman-Steis

to anyone with any labels, I could just be whoever I wanted to be in moments that I was there. By this time in my everyday belief systems, I had come to pray regularly, by this I mean constant conversations with God and retraining the co-pilot within myself to believe in love grace and mercy and not fear. I had gotten past the infatuation and honeymoon and finally had a deep grounded relationship with God and the god force inside me. Church could finally be a new experience for me, and I wanted to sit with this for a while. I had watched folks weekly and got reacquainted with the ritual process of a 2000-year-old routine in faith. I sometimes questioned what my take was from this new activity. I came to realize that I was going to just use the hour every week to be without labels to exist just as who I was for that week, that moment. To enjoy others around me and to be of service to anyone who asked for assistance. I did make a few friends that we had coffee together after service every week, but even within those connections I remained free of labels. I did not define myself as this or that and just let them see me as who they saw me as. It was a wonderful thing, and it built a greater love in me for church folk, after all I was one of them now.

Just as a routine set it, as always, change was just around the corner. The Vicar would be leaving and heading south to a new church and my son was working every Sunday making it impossible for him to get to church weekly. Yet I continued to attend in my bliss of just being. In the liturgical church they have a system and best practice for everything, I mean everything. Its so tidy in its approach to systems that it sometimes comes across as broken in some ways. They would put together a discernment committee to find a new Vicar for the church and apparently this search could take well over a year. This would provide an opportunity for some other Vicars to come in weekly to give service. For the first few months we had several different folks leading service. That was fun. Some of them got super loud and excited, some created the best napping environment for some much-needed rest. Either way I enjoyed them all and the responses of the folks there listen. I saw it as a huge social experiment that I could be apart of weekly. It was such an exciting time.

Finally, they located an interim priest to stay at the church until a new one could be found and brought in. If someone asked me what I thought of this new Vicar I would simply say, "well she's even." And that is exactly what she was, even, consistent and steady. No loud yelling from the pulpit or overly obnoxious scenes of the holy spirit, but good solid message of grace and mercy, an explanation of God as love, only. There are a few things that happened during her stay there that I am going to point out because it was the beginning of me waking up to a seedier underside to the church, one that needed to be addressed, one that would change me forever by pushing me into a new definition to myself.

During the time that Vicar Interim was acting my appendix burst. I became extremely ill and spent some time in the hospital. I was absent from church for a few weeks while on the mend. Once I returned home a friend from the church, Nan, reached out and asked why I had missed service and I explained what had happened. As always, with a good church member, she contacted the Vicar and told them I was ill. I was then contacted by a gentleman that offered to bring me food, which I declined. I was also contacted by the Vicar and asked if I needed anything. I again declined. I was not at the church for any services and I really had everything I needed to regain my health and be well again. She seemed a bit put off that I declined but that's not my issue to address. Nan continued to call me almost every evening to check on things and see when I would return to church. During one of these calls, she caught me in a vulnerable moment. I had received the bill for the surgery. Due to a recently starting my own business I did not have health insurance. This bill being over 30k would drain my bank account for the most part. This had me a bit in a way, and yet glad I had the savings to pay the bill. When she called that evening I explained, in my frenzy, that I was strapped financially over this surgery and I wasn't sure how it would work out. I was just venting. When we got off the phone she did what every good church Christian does and went into action calling folks and telling them I need help. Gossip for the sake of love always amuses me, it's a real head shaker.

When I returned to church, the following week, after the service I was summoned into the Vicars office. I have to say I felt as if I was being called into the school principal. I did not care for the fact that suddenly I felt as if I was a child needing guidance. Its set me on edge a bit. Here I am minding my own business back to church happy to be alive and on the mend and I am being requested to go see the Vicar? Why? But then I thought to myself, you are being ridiculous she probably just wants to see how you're feeling. The long hallway/ramp leading to coffee hour goes right past the Vics office, I will swing by say I'm fine and move along. I get to the door tap on its ad enter. "What's Up? Interim Vicar?" She said come in have a seat. I was told you may be having some financial issues. I said What?! She said oh? I was told you may be struggling with something and I wanted to let you know the church could help if you need the help? Hang on... I thought to myself. You are calling me in here based on someone else's word of it and haven't asked how I am feeling, yet want to throw money at me as a possible maybe problem? My mind at this point is racing with next steps and what to dos, not to mention that I feel more than embarrassed for no damn good reason. I felt less then. I also think she really enjoyed the notion that she may be able to help me, it brought her satisfaction. I stored that information in my mind to think about later. I needed to answer her and not be an asshole about it. I said after a pause. "I thank you for your concern however I am not in need of any assistance from the church. I am not certain as to who is talking about what, but I am fine, I do thank you for your concern."

I knew exactly who it was, and I also knew that in all of this not one bit of harm was meant to anyone. I was going to leave it there and be done with it. I will say the Vicar looked somewhat disappointed that I declined her offer. She stated, "If your need should change and the church can help you please reach out to Kit and let her now and I will leave notes to ensure they help you." The Vicar would be rolling out soon so the new Vicar could come in and she wanted to ensure provision was made just in case. I thanked her and awkwardly rushed out of the office. I could not wait to get out of there, what the fuck had just happened. I was going to go to coffee hour and address the source. I knew she meant no harm, but I wanted to reassure her that she caught me in a moment and that all was well.

I went got my coffee and sat down at the table. Before I could even open my mouth Nan energetically said, "Did you go see the Vicar? Did she help you? I know I may have stepped into your business, but I sure do hope they are able to assist you. I spent so much time this week worried about you and I reached out hoping they could help you." I took one look into her eyes and realized that she had no malice or intent to do harm, that she was loving me as a friend and wanted good things to happen. I said, "I am not sure they can help me with anything at this time." She said, 'you didn't turn down the help did you? I don't want to look foolish or be sneered at for making a fuss and find out you turned down the help. What will they think, they may think I was lying about your troubles?" I looked at her for a long time as she went on about looking foolish when trying to care for a friend. I pondered where this fear was coming from, was there something happening in the church I had not yet recognized, with regard to gossip and its destructive ways? Why would anyone fault her for caring? She was truly troubled. I said to her, "Nan please relax, the Vicar asked that I think about it and if something came up to contact Kit. I will give it some thought and see what if anything I may need help with." When I left the church that day I was truly baffled about the whole mess. I learned many things though. I learned that I should never tell Nan if I am upset or need assistance if I don't want the church to know. I learned that there may be an underlying issue surrounding gossip and its attitudes within the church. And I also learned that pride is a nasty little ego driven varmint and what was I going to do about it. So, I did what any decent respectable person would do. I thought about it and came up with a plan that would make everyone look good and teach me a much-needed lesson in pride. I wrote Kit an email a week later and stated that I had talked with the Vicar and she said if I needed anything you all could help. I explained that I needed help and what help I needed and with a few adjustments Kit made it happen. Easy as that I was told to go the church on a day and time and pick up a check. Huh? It was humiliating to ask for money and it be brought before a group of folks that you know would speak about it to other folks, of course solely out of love and pity. It was a perfect lesson in pride. It fixed everything. I got the help and it made Nan look like she was a great friend. The church got to be the hero and I got a framed check to mount on my wall to remind me that when someone gets to the point in which they have to ask for money, allowing strangers into their personal affairs it is a tough time. It was not easy to ask for help and I work in a field that folks ask for help daily, until that moment I did not know the struggle to the spirit when one must beg. I determined in that moment I would never judge another person panhandling or asking for help again. In that moment I knew one thing about folks needing assistance. It does not matter if the person needs help or what I might think they are going to spend the money on or where, the point of giving to someone is not about them at all, its about me and my willingness to help, its about my heart to give.

I never used or a cashed the check, the new vicar came to me about six months maybe a year later and asked about the check. I explained to her that I still had the check and that I was not going to use it, but she could not have it back but was more than welcome to cancel it. I explained it was an important lesson. She said, "do you want to share." I said "no" and walked away. I wondered many times, thinking back on this, if I have ever made anyone feel the way I did in asking for money from someone. I don't know but I do know I make sure as much as possible I do not make them feel this way now and if I can avoid someone having to ask or feel like they are begging I will go the extra mile to ensure they are comfortable. Working in the disability and aging field for 27 years I am asked almost daily for financial help and resources, and it has changed how I do everything when it comes to client support.

The second occurrence with this interim Vicar was a lesson in communication. I taught a course on communications at the local community college for several years as a part of new staff hires and required state certifications. I know we all have deficits in communications, but I do think myself to be a pretty decent listener, (could do better) and an even better explainer of all things Dawn. Remember back in chapter one I explained that I had a desire to become a priest? Well, I had sat in the church long enough this go around to have that little bugger of a nudge get up under my skin again. It nagged and nagged at me, always with that one burning question. "Who preaches to the preacher, who teaches the teacher?" It became so constant that I actually got my butt up during coffee hour one Sunday morning and went to Interim Vicar and said, "do you have a minute?" I sat down and explained that I had this happen as a child and it was back again, and I just could not seem to get it to GO AWAY. She chuckled and said, "We call that the hounds of heaven." We talked briefly and she said how bout we set up time to meet for a few weeks and then gave me a book recommendation. She felt it would help me as I felt I was not the proper material for a becoming a priest. She suggested

Nadia Bolz-Weber book called *Pastrix*. I also mentioned I was not interested in the role, she seemed to ignore that. I did read the book and I did understand why she suggested it as Nadia seemed and unlikely person to take on the role of priest.

For about two or three weeks we met and discussed this constant nudge. We talked about steps to become, we talked about some alternatives to becoming as she recommended some class as well as suggested me to serve on the alter again. I agreed to both. The class would be fun. Learning random stuff that doesn't seem useful is a specialty of mine. Serving on the alter was cool. I love to read with inflection when reading the Bible. To many people read just so mechanically that it doesn't make the bible folks seem as if they were ever real. So, doing the readings is fun. Several other parishioners liked me reading also and when I stopped doing it questioned why. We couldn't find the class being held anywhere so I just let it go. During our talked Interim Vicar started to seem impatient and finally said she would leave a note for the new Vicar and I should continue to discuss this. I explained that I didn't want to discuss it anymore I just wanted it to go away. How could we make it go away? She seemed frazzled by that statement. I explained, "well that's why I came to you in the first place, I thought we were having these talks so that you could help it go away and I could get back to my quiet existence in the back pew on Sundays." Completely frustrated she looked and said I will leave some notes and you do what you think you should. So, I left thinking, my God, this is never going to go away and the interim priest can't even help me. Before I left, I turned and thanked her for her time and effort realizing now that we had both been wasting time as I was seeking, and end and she was testing a possible beginning. I got rid of the nagging by taking an online course and becoming ordained over the intra webs, apparently its not rocket science to become a priest its just paper and a few bucks and instant gratification. I was obedient to the leading and bam I'm done nothing more needed to be done. Famous last words.

I did learn in the first few years that communications in a church group setting can be tricky. It seems when folks walk past the threshold, they suddenly put on an invisible shroud of ownership to each other. It gives the outward appearance of a global sort of family. I found within the first four or so years of being back in attendance that being very clear about what your intent is within your conversation is important other wise you could be talking about planting a fruit tree in your back yard and the next week get 20 fruit baskets delivered to your house because someone felt lead to get you fruit without you having to wait for it to grow. So for the most part I listened and spoke only to a very few about personal things or life stories.

I continued to serve and read and appreciated my quiet non defined moments sitting in the pew every week. I liked this church thing this time around. I helped a couple of the ladies start a soup kitchen, one of the girls had a sister who needed benefits help and I was able to assist her through the process. Another woman I invited to a virtual dementia tour and walked through it with her to better understand her husband, shoveled driveways and cut lawns. Helped with projects here and there. When someone came up missing for a while, I would call them or pop in and see them. Never once telling anyone what I was doing or had done, never once looking for recognition. Just being whatever was needed in the capacity that I had to help. It was good and it was free. Joe eventually got baptized and church became a part of weekly life, I have to laugh about it now because it was the last place I ever thought myself to participate as an adult and at my own choice. But it was good to see and feel how far I had come to heal old wounds and gain a higher level of independence in my understanding of the church and why people rely on it. But more healing of all old wounds was on the way.

Dawn Feldman-Steis

Independence in the Church Community

For if you remain completely silent at this time, relief and deliverance will arise for the Jews from another place, but you and your fathers house will perish. Yet who knows whether you have come to the kingdom for such a time as this? **NKJV (The names and timeline of events in this chapter have been changed to protect the guilty.)**

The new Vicar finally made it to church. She was a young girl, almost childlike. So very new to the position of priest that she was like a deer in the headlights. She nestled in and for the first few years gained comfort into her new title. In those first years she cried during sermons and baptisms, as if she were ministering to herself and getting caught up in the awesomeness of role she had taken on, and who doesn't cry a bit at baptisms. Some folks took issue with this crying priest, but I saw it as humility and a great gift to a young minister. Many of us struggle with staying humble but true humility that is certainly a gift, a gift that would eventually wain for this young priest.

I had stopped my service to the church as a LEM and had also stopped reading on Sundays as I recognized that I made the priest somewhat nervous. I wasn't sure why and I questioned her concerning this several times as I wanted to make sure it was her thing and not something I had done without notice. I stopped these things because I am not in attendance or in activities of the church to make anyone nervous or uncomfortable, it is not my interest. So I removed myself for her comfort.

About two years into her signing on something started to change. Maybe it was confidence and true personalities began to show, maybe there was personal concerns weighing the priest down, maybe I had become more involved in the church and so more aware? What ever the change it was not a good shift by any means and if it was personal to the priest it was not my business. I began to witness the priest berate some of the older members of the church. They would ask a question and she would snap back with a, "Sit down before you break a hip." Or a "No I ask you to do this, do what I ask or don't do it at all." At one point she insisted that everyone clap to a hymn so we could feel the spirit which became an awkward untimed mess. That was the thing that pushed me to write the first letter. I remember struggling that Sunday evening, praying and saying to god "I don't want to write a letter." But the insistence of the spirit won out and I wrote a letter and sent by email. This letter would be the first of about five and I found myself fighting with God about being the modern-day Paul. That was Paul's gig he wrote letters and went to prison and then wrote more letters. Its funny to me looking back on it now simply because I just really do not care for the Paul we have come to know in the bible.

Each time I wrote a letter there seemed to be a correction for a time and then right back to being unpleasant. Several of us would take notice of her need to isolate from folks and not be a part of things if she didn't have to be. We would talk about it and then agree to pray, and I would get nagged to write a letter. Sometimes it was just a letter of my own journey with God and a high five or leg up your doing good hang in there kinda thing. It was uncomfortable for me as I really just was in church to appreciate the time unidentified, with no labels. This letter thing was messing with my peace and happiness. But it was only once in awhile and better to follow the lead then to have that nagging. Come to think about it I really didn't care what the priest was thinking I more cared that I was listening and following the spirit. I also cared that folks were being injured and I hate that, intentional or unintentional it just rubs me until I act.

I decided in the fall of my last year at the church that I would go to the church retreat. Work had been overwhelming our nation was changing and unsettled and I was told that the retreats are always so relaxing. I was really thinking it would be a change of pace and give me time away from people to refocus and get closer to creation and God. The first night was spent waiting for folks to role in and get settled and later that evening playing games and having light refreshments and drinks (of all kinds) while we get to know each other a bit. I realized at this moment that the weekend was about to be tricky for me. Because folks would want to define you based on answers to questions and the types of activities planned. You know, those getting to know you games. The first night I was sitting with one of my closer church friends, we enjoyed kayaking and hanging out together for the occasional happy hour. We were playing the game UNO with a group of people, priest included. My friend, being from Germany, was explaining the rules of the game to me with regard to the large group playing and the priest chimed in and said, "No that's not the rule, you are in America now. You have to follow the American rules." Now when some one says such a thing it can be hurtful but not intended to be hurtful, but when someone says it more then once well now we have a letter writing kind of problem. The priest said this same sentence four times to my friend within less than five minutes. She repeated so much so that it became seriously hurtful and the game ended. People laughed and never thought once how that might be affecting others around and I believe they laughed only because the priest said it. Anyone other than the priest and I think it would have been taken seriously and addressed immediately. I felt the energy in the room change and then the silence came and then the laughs. Laughs mostly to try and shrug off the awkwardness of the moment. I got quiet said nothing and saying nothing in times like this is equally wrong. We all went to our rooms and I still said nothing. The next morning, I met up with my friend for breakfast and as we were walking into the dining hall several folks who had been with us the night before came up to my friend and said, "You know you're in America now, right? You know the American rules to Uno now, right?" As they laughed and thought it was funny. I could feel each word go through my friend like a dagger. She quipped back "Oh yea I got it." But she was hurt, and I knew it and I said nothing again. I went for a long walk alone that morning and skipped out on whatever everyone was doing. I needed to process my next steps. I was disappointed in myself and concerned for the message coming across from church members. I went to my friend later in the afternoon and apologized that I didn't stand up and say anything and that I was sorry that folks felt free to be so unkind. She explained that she had to deal with a lot of behavior like that since she moved to this country. Not only because she was from another country but because she was from Germany. I think that's terrible and I was more than upset with myself for not speaking up. So, I went to find the priest to discuss and thought maybe it could get rectified before dinner. I could not find the priest and when I did there was always someone needing something. So, I decided to wait and discuss it when there was time to talk about it. Sunday everyone headed back, since I road with my friend we discussed it on the way home, she stated she wasn't going to go to another retreat, this bothered me, but I understood. I didn't really ever want to go to another retreat either, because it is hard to be around that many people all weekend when you work with people all week. By the way it was not relaxing at all it was busy and non-stop.

By that evening I was so unnerved by the hurt of my friend and the many instances of hearing and seeing unkind words to others that I wrote the priest. I let her know her actions were painful as well as it gave permission to others to act unkindly also. I asked questions concerning other families in the church, would she have talked the same way to our minority families or new families coming into the church. I asked that she speak with my friend and apologize and suggested that she might apologize publicly since she hurt her publicly. The priest wrote back and stated she had talked with my friend and was not aware of the outcome and hurt that she felt over the weekend. My friend, who I bcc'd on the email wrote me and thanked me as she never thought anyone would do something like that for her. All felt right with the world again it was back to business as usual. We all had an opportunity to grow and learn from each other and to recognize the need for correction and change.

I will say the whole thing left me cautious and suddenly wide awake to those around me. I most definitely was not going to get personal with this group. I briefly thought I would share my 25-year clean anniversary with the group and ask for prayer, that was suddenly off the table. I was seeing something shift in the church, was it the priest, or was it always there? More importantly I was wide awake to the folks in the church that would follow any leading as long as the leading came from the priest. As long as they were in the cool club. It is truly scary to watch folks give up their own moral compass to be in with the leader. Pack mentality was showing its ugly head again and I needed to stay awake.

A few months later we would hold our silent action fund raising event. This was the start of the craziest church nonsense I have ever seen or been apart of. I had donated several boxes of wine for the event and had brief discussion with the priest the night before on whether the donations could still be made. I dropped the wine off in the morning and returned with four friends that evening to have a great night with friends and church friends combined. I wasn't much of bringing friends to church. It gives people reason to talk and gossip even though you have never said anything about yourself. For never defining myself I was about to be defined in ways I never thought folks could think up. Some funny and some hurtful but all lies and gossip.

When we entered the auction, we received two tickets for wine and our papers for the auction. We went in and mingled and started to look around. Got our quarter full tumblers of wine and finger foods. As my friends settled in at a table, I did my typical waltz around the room talking to folks and seeing how everyone was. As I spoke with folks, they would give me their wine tickets. I didn't ask for the tickets, folks would just hand them to me if I could use them. There was nothing posted about limitations on wine tickets. I took the tickets to accept the act of kindness knowing full well my friends could use them if they wanted more. As I went to see my friend from retreat sitting just outside the kitchen door, I took notice to the church sexton in the kitchen watching my friend give me two more tickets. I then observed the priest come into the kitchen and the sexton turning to her giving a nod in my direction and them both staring. What I saw was the sexton telling the priest that I was getting extra tickets from people. I took the tickets from my friend while they watched, and slipped them in my pocket with the others, turned and gave the audience in the kitchen a nod to let them know I was watching also, then turned and walked over to talk to my friends Joe and Phyliss. They also would give me more tickets that I would slip into my pocket, not giving it any thought.

After finishing up with them and discussing next items to be bid on I started back to my friends. As I walked across the room JD, the lead organizer to the night's events, came and stopped me. She said, "Dawn?! How's your night going?" I said, "Great, have you tried the chocolate wine I brought yet?" She stated she hadn't had a chance yet. JD then asked if I was intoxicated? I asked a bit taken back by the question, "Do I look intoxicated?", she said "No". JD then asked how many tickets I had. I responded by saying how many tickets am I supposed to have? She said two. So, I said, "then I have two." I then asked JD directly, "What is this about?" She responded without hesitation that the priest had come to her and stated that I was getting tickets from people and that I was intoxicated. Again, I reassured JD that I was not intoxicated and that I was the designated driver in my group of people. I said, "I tell ya what, I have these two tickets JD how bout I buy you a chocolate wine with one and I buy a wine for the priest with the other and let her know I am not intoxicated? That way everyone is back on the same page." JD said well that sounds like a great idea. So, we walked to the wine bar asked for the two drinks, JD had hers and I turned and headed toward the priest with the other. The priest saw me coming and she knew I was on my way, she had a look of, Oh the cats out of the bag, on her face. You know that look folks give when they have been caught in doing something and they are trying to figure their next steps in the next moments. The priest knew I would stand up for myself she also knew I do not do gossip and yet she had been gossiping. Not only had she been gossiping, she had added a lie to the story by stating I was intoxicated. I walked up to her and simply went to hand her the glass of wine and before I could say anything, she started flailing her arms in the air in a louder voice saying you are just work to me, I have to work in the morning this is my workplace. I stood there for a moment baffled at the response. I expected the flight or fight response to kick in, I just didn't think it was going to be so oh I don't know high school like? She scampered off while mumbling and continuing her scene, I shrugged my shoulders and walked away, as a few folks stood there laughing at the scene. You see the priest had no idea what I was going to say or do. She didn't even really know if I was coming to talk to her or the gentlemen standing behind her? What she did know was that she had listened to gossip in the kitchen drawn assumptions from those talks and went to another parishioner to handle her bidding with a full-blown lie. When she saw me coming toward her, she reacted to the guilt of her actions not to anything I was doing at all.

I went back to my group a bit embarrassed by the scene but more confused to the reaction as the ability to adult for this priest was not something that came easy to her. I left that night and dropped off my friends, it was somewhat early. I then went home and sent a text message to the priest. I had, had it with her constant patronization of parishioners. I had addressed it over and over and now she was going to attempt to come at me? So, I sent a text message that said, "Priest I am usually very patient, and I have been more than patient, however if you raise your voice to me again in anger or as if I am a child, I will call you out during a sermon. You are a visitor of this church. You work for the church the church does not work for you. No one should be talked down to or treated poorly. Fly right priest!" Now I am not saying that what I sent was the right thing to do. IT was truly sent out of anger and I just wanted this priest to be better, to do better, and to be kind to all of the parishioners. If I had to do it over, I probably would wait until the next day and found a more political approach, but I had been watching this priest get increasingly nasty with folks and it just pissed me off, so I had a moment. The priest came back and suggested that if I had an issue that we should meet in her office and discuss it, I thought to myself; again, with another meeting, why? I came back and explained that I would not meet with her again. She had requested several meetings with me over the last couple years in which we didn't really discuss anything. I'd show up we talk about stupid shit or my son we would pray about something and I would leave. Hindsight folks, oh hindsight... I explained that meeting with her solved nothing in the past and that she would be at this church for a very short time compared to the fact that I would be here for years to come and I was not going to be pushed around by anyone. Famous last words. Sunday after church during coffee hour I went to the priest and handed her the twenty plus tickets given to me the night before and stated, "Gossip was a dangerous thing, judgement without knowledge is even worse." Later down the road the priest translates this sentence to "glass is broken." I thought to myself, "WTF does that mean?" How do you get glass is broken from gossip is a dangerous thing? Clearly one of the issues with this priest was hearing loss. At that point I shrugged my shoulders and I saw the incident as over and maybe she would self-correct maybe not, but I needed to get quiet again and figure on my next steps. Would I stay in the church would I leave what was my spirit compass telling me?

Come Monday I received an email from Junior and Senior Wardens. (Note that Junior is listed first because I still hold respect for this woman, no matter her involvement. She was used. She was manipulated and I feel sorry for her.) Junior requested that I come into the church for a meeting with her and Senior. I responded by asking about what? Junior responded that it was to discuss concerns from an incident that happened at the silent auction. Uh Oh, I was being called to the principal's office, again… lol, but I am a grown ass adult now so my answer was, "I have already addressed the incident that took place, and I will not discuss it with you or anyone else, thank you and have a great day." Of course, I am sure this stirred the pot, but I don't have to meet with anyone at any time if I don't want to. Wednesday comes along and I receive another email form Senior, she states that they are having interviews for the organist that evening and looking for those on the discernment committee to attend if they can. Being on the discernment committee I asked if they had new resumes or if we were working off the ones we already had. Senior responded by saying "they were using the resumes we had, interviews will start at 6pm see ya there." So, I showed up for the interviews walked into the foyer of the church, it was very dimly lit and before I could turn around both Junior and Senior had come behind me blocking the main doors. I said "hey what's up? Where are we meeting?" Knowing full well they had set me up. They said we want to talk with you about what happened. I said, then you talk and tell me what happened. They said you were inappropriate with the priest. I said what are you talking about? They accused me of being threatening to the priest. I said they would have to prove that. I said, "you mean when I cussed her out?" They said, "yes." I never cussed at the priest not once in this whole mess, so there's that lie or maybe they were going from a lie told to them by the priest. They said, "we have talked with the bishop and you and the priest must stay away from each other and you are not to participate in any extra activities with the church that the priest is in the lead on." It was dark and I was blocked in with no way out. I informed them that what they were doing was not scriptural. That the bible lays out the steps to take when difficulties arise in the group. Junior looked at me and said, "what do you mean?" I tried not to laugh in her face, but it has always been my experience in organized beliefs that those in charge don't know their own rules to follow. I quoted Mathew 18 to both of them and they stated, "Oh I am not familiar with that verse." I said, "get familiar you are in a role that you should at least know the basics." I kindly but sternly asked that they both move away from the door's and let me pass. Realizing that they had set this whole thing up as an ambush without full information, I walked past them and out the door. I then went to a book study at my friend's house organized by the church, was never much for anyone telling me what to do. I was told at the book group that they had intended to ambush me at this friend's house and not the church. This friend being the same friend I stood up for just a few months before. The book was "The Shack" and about forgiveness and I was super pissed off by the time I got to her home. When I went in, her and one other person were already discussing things. I went in and told them both what had just happened. They were both shocked. (or where they) About that time another member of the tribe of church leadership came in, we will call her Kit. We were still talking about what happened and she acted like she knew nothing, later I would find out things to be vastly different. Oh, church folk are so predictable when they get into their schoolgirl ways. This night would be the beginning of a six-month long beratement and targeted abuse toward me, not just by Junior and Senior but the entire church leadership team, with the priest hiding in the shadows calling the next shots but never having the courage to step forward. I reached out to leadership outside of the church and had meetings with them and took a witness with me to explain my concerns and what I was seeing within the church. The gentlemen that met with me, his only response while we met was that he was shocked that this was about the church for me and Joe, and he explained that for the priest it was very personal. He repeated that several times through out our meeting that the issues at hand were not church related for the priest but personal. Finally, I stopped him and said what are you talking about why would they be personal? Its not personal it a church wide issue and it needs corrected. After he left my friend Joe suggested that maybe it was personal for the priest and that is why it had been such a volatile response to my calling her out. That maybe she was a woman scorned. I stated to Joe at some point it would take a lot of assumption on the priest and church leadership to take that angle as I have never self-identified in the church with any labels. I had never really given it any thought, but the idea seemed to fit the actions and she was using an entire group to do her bidding.

I had actually gone on mission and travel for six weeks during this six-month period of time and when I returned it started all over again. Two things to note here. I could have left the church at any time however I did not feel released to do so yet and it was the church my son was baptized in. Two they could have just let things go and moved on when I returned. Oh, stories went through the church like wildfire. They took my sons name off the prayer list when he was deployed and told everyone that he was kicked out of the military to justify doing so. One of the girls told parishioners that I asked to sleep naked in a field in a sleeping bag with her and her wife at a retreat. I chuckled and responded by saying, "I don't go barefoot in my own home let alone get naked in the forest with strangers" ... and we all had a good laugh. Another said I hit on a lady right in front of him at the retreat, apparently telling someone that you like their dress or their hair looks great while standing in the lunch line, is hitting on them. But more importantly there was a huge assumption being made and I just wonder where it came from. I went from being a quiet unidentified parishioner three rows from the back to becoming a filthy demon spawn with lesbian tendencies. It seemed that maybe my fried Joe was on to something when he suggested that the priest was acting like a woman scorned. Why was I suddenly being labeled with any sort of sexual identity by the church? Why was my personal life suddenly a topic to discuss? More importantly, why was I suddenly given so much power?

I went from being huggable every week to being sneered at. I realized there was a leak in the ship, and it was letting gossip pour in at alarming rates. And yet I soldiered on and continued to sit in prayer for them all, every week. I did make a few posts on Facebook here and there concerning churches in general and the misuse of power. I did call the priest out on her sermons of love and forgiveness by using the churches Facebook page. Yea so I pushed back a bit, I stood up in anger to attempt to show injustice. I wasn't going to be controlled or manipulated and I wanted it to be known. We don't always do the correct things all the time, it felt like a way for self-preservation right or wrong it relieved some of the tensions. Its ok to be angry if we use it to push toward correction and truth.

I went away again for a couple weeks and when I returned, I noticed on the sign up for anything church board that there were a few things coming up that the priest was not going be in charge of or involved in. The rule was, that I had been following to a T, (which by the way I think made them angrier that I followed the rules than if I had broken them) that I could not attend anything that the priest was leading or attending. No problem I will wait because what I know is that she is not a joiner and does not want to be involved with much and I am not interested in being involved in anything she is leading. So here is my chance to try again. I asked the organizer to the Church picnic if they still needed help on the grills. He said, "yes sign up" and so I did. There was also a meeting Sunday morning for the block party led by two of the vestry. So, I thought let me go to that and so I did. The priest, as immature as she was, almost busted a vein when she saw me sitting in the meeting. A meeting she was not participating in and suddenly had time to sit in on. She got up and paced out in the hall and then came back in the room several times, it was quite the show. And again, I could feel the power of the demon spawn welling up inside me getting ready to stand and devour them... lol Nah, I'm just kidding I grinned and continued the meeting then went to service as if nothing happened because that's what you do at church when you're an adult. Later that evening while reading at home I received a call from Mr. Picnic, he stated he wasn't sure what was going on but that I could not work the grills unless I called the office first. I had to contact the office. I said do you have a number or email to contact the office? He said he wasn't sure what they meant by that and that he was sorry for what ever was going on. Poor guy was more baffled than I was. Mr. Picnic was always a kind man. I hung up and thought to myself, interesting, and then I prayed and asked when I might be done with this church, that a little direction would be nice in the next steps of this mess, can I get a sign? Not yet, wait, a faint whisper said… and so I prayed.

I sent an email to Junior and Senior the next day asking what the issue was and why they would continue this madness and pettiness for months now. They continued to repeat the same thing over and over throughout the months. You sent inappropriate text messages and emails to the priest. I asked for copies of those things over and over and they provided nothing. I waited I knew that the letters I had sent to the priest about the church in general had some pretty sensitive and personal info in them. I kept asking for the proof of the allegations and then… Senior snorted back in an email, "You did send those messages and emails I know I have read them all." I could only assume at this point that they meant my letters concerning the church and I viewed this now as a breach of confidentiality from the priest. She was spreading my personal stories, around to people with out my knowledge or permission. I was instantly livid and hurt all at the same time. I felt emotionally raped and found myself back in old clothes again, but this time was different, I wasn't the kid in the art closet anymore and mom wasn't going to show up and make it better. When Senior, out of anger and self-pride, boasted of her reading my personal stories it was as if a bubble burst over the whole mess. There it was the very root of the problem, the manipulation that creates the gossip and lies, it was that moment that everyone is yelling all at the same time and then suddenly Senior belts out I have read them, all of them; and a hush comes over everyone, a still silence. Everyone knows the wrong in it and everything just stops. I wrote back and said I would be in touch later that this conversation was now at an end. I waited a day then wrote an email of which I included everyone on. I explained my disappointment in the breach of confidentiality by the priest and I requested that we seek mediation services. I even offered at this point to pay for half the cost to correct this situation. I wanted a meeting that would be fair and service both sides. I was ignored.

Dawn Feldman-Steis

Come Sunday I went through service as normal praying during service to be released from this madness and asking that grace preserve whatever remained in this parish for those unaffected. I did not take communion this day during service, instead I went to Junior after the service and I requested to receive communion from a lay minister as this would keep in accordance with their rules in keeping the priest away from me, and at this point I wanted nothing more. I explained that due to the breach of confidentiality and the feelings of being emotionally raped by this priest I did not want communion from her. Junior agreed this would be a solid outcome and said she would ask someone to get me communion that day. I received communion privately from a woman that I once assisted through a virtual dementia tour for her husband. She was trying to better understand his condition and I told her about the course. I actually ended up staying and holding her hand through most of the tour. It is a scary perspective to put yourself into a loved one's shoes especially if that loved one has a terrible disease or condition. This woman also served on the vestry and had been misinformed of the circumstances. It was hard for her to give me communion and she wept a bit. She seemed confused and fearful all at the same time. I thanked her and told her this would all be over soon and someday would be nothing but a memory if even that. I went to junior again and requested that I continue to get communion through the lay ministry and if it had to be served to me from home or outside the church that was ok also but that some arrangement should be made. She agreed at the time. She even confirmed by email during the week that it was set, and I would receive communion from another lay minister.

Next Sunday came and I made sure to be early, most Sundays I would sit in the church before service and process timesheets for staff, it was quite and a good time for focus. Not one church leader addressed me about communion. During the passing of the peace,

I noticed the priest discussing something with Junior and Senior. I figured if there was going to be an issue with communion, they would let me know before I got in line, right? So, I assumed it was as discussed and got in line. As I went up through line I looked to Junior and with an inquisitive gesture put a hand up as if to say are we good, she looked back and shrugged her shoulders like she wasn't sure. She seemed baffled and a bit bewildered. I continued on in the line and the priest, with a smirk on her face, attempted to hand me the host. I said in a low voice but stern, "No." and moved along through the line and back to my seat. It was then apparently clear that this priest was not going to stop her assault as she made the decision to weaponize communion. And I was not taking communion from an emotional rapist or abusive priest. At that time Junior came back to my pew and said do you want to step outside and discuss what just happened? I said no thanks, I know what just happened. She went back to her seat. At the end of the service, I went through the receiving line out the church and around to the ramp that led to coffee hour.

A vestry member, who should not be involved, stood by the priest as protection to the priest from the evil spawn that is Dawn for the past few Sundays. I took pictures of this craziness to show folks how crazy they had become, blind really. This vestry member actually stood at the end of my pew one Sunday and I could not figure out why, later I came to be told that they had spread terrible lies about me threatening the priest and this was their way of showing off for their stories. They looked so stupid acting out some made-up play of events in their minds. A real-life drama club.

I was one of the last people out of the church as I got caught up talking with someone. As I walked down the ramp I watched as Junior and Senior worked to position themselves by and outside door in the foyer but close to the hallway as to not miss me pass by them. I assessed and thought to myself, "oh I am not doing this shit today; I will bring my grievances to the heads of the church tomorrow." I purposefully walked past and just when I thought I was out of the way I heard Senior call my name. "Dawn." I turn and walked back, and she says, "Would you like to step out of the church and discuss communion today?" (I thought to myself, why do these folks insist on talking to me alone and without witnesses?) I said "No, there is no need for discussion, it is clear the priest does not want to follow her own rules and for her to manipulate communion as a weapon has got to be some new low for this church. Can I ask why you both insist in a constant attempt to isolate me away from others?" She said, "Well the priest does not want to set a precedent that others may follow." I said, "Yet we have a lay ministry that could come to my home or meet me elsewhere and not show a precedent at all. Do you not both see how you're being manipulated. You are just pawns." I turned to walk away, and I hear Junior say, "What is the big deal why can't you just get communion from the priest?" I stop turned and walked back and said, "Have you not been paying attention? Did you not read the emails from Senior this week? Do you not understand that this priest has spiritually and emotionally raped me, and you have stood there and watched her do it maybe even assisted her with it?" I turned to Senior and said, "And you should know better you as the leader of the vestry, you have exposed not only your priest but your church to consequences beyond your imagination with regard to exposing this breach. What is wrong with you? Where is your leadership?" I was then ushered into a Sunday school classroom out of the eye of folks that had no idea what was happening. In a brief moment there was approximately 10 people all blocking the door to get out. They semi circled around me everyone yelling a different version of what they heard about me, at me. It was chaos but I remained focused on Senior. I remained focused because she knew better than to promote this kind of behavior and instead precipitated it and enjoyed her role in doing so. As we were arguing the point at hand the priest walked smoothly into the room up behind the back of Senior and stared directly at me while she whispered into the ear of Senior telling her what to say next. I recognized in the priest's eyes that same look that the pastor had so many years before when he was waiting for me to cry while doling out punishment. One person yelled out I want a meeting lets get to the bottom of this, I said "Yes let's have a meeting right now I will go get the paperwork and emails from my car and we can all sit down and meet right now." Junior and Senior in unison rang out a quick, "Nooo!." To having a meeting.

As I turned back to make eye contact with the priest who was acting like some hateful high school cheerleader that didn't win the cheer competition, a vestry member, Kit, who was once a friend came up behind me put her arm around my lower back and said let's get you out of here. As we walked past the mass of people blocking the doorway the priest stopped us and said, "and don't call me a piece of shit again." The shock and horror in the group as people gasped and one said," Did she really say that?" The priest replied, "Well Judy Nosely said she said that." I turned around to face her and said, "This started with gossip and you're ending it with more gossip, you are such a liar." I was shaken from so many people having me blocked into the room and yelling. I was angry and could not drive yet, I met up with friends at a table and sat to have a cup of coffee and calm myself until I was safe to drive. They stayed by me and tried to provide comfort. Junior and Senior came up to me at the table and said, "We want you to leave." I said, "No, I am not leaving until I finish my coffee." They said we will call the police, "I said, "call the police, do what you have to just get away from me and stop instigating further issues."

I sat there for about 30 minutes and regained my steadiness. No police came. I said quietly in my spirit, "Now can I go? Please lord?" I realized just then what Jesus must have felt like when the

Pharisees rose against him. Those that showed him so much love at the beginning turned so coldly to accuse and condemn. Just as sure as I witnessed the betrayal of Judas in that classroom, I was coming through something more... something bigger. AS I stood up and took my coffee cup to the dishwasher, I knew it would be the last time, I realized that I was brushing the dirt from my feet. God was telling me it was now time to let go. AS I said goodbye to friends and turned my back to enemies and walked that long walk through the parking lot to my truck, I was being set free. I wasn't a child leaving the office walking down that long trailer hall learning to be angry and alone. I wasn't an angry teenager ready to condemn God to an earthy grave, I was an adult broken and transformed, pulled from the cross and in the midst of the pain and confusion of it all I was finding healing. Healing from all the pain through all the years of doctrine and church law, defining the course of belief. Each step I took away from the church was step closer to who I was becoming. Each tear that fell that day was a piece of that shell I built so many years before melting away, falling off of my definition and becoming my history. I was not angry, I was not raging, I was broken and rung out, but I was free and new in every step. I was weary and tired, beaten and bruised and yet freed to rise up into something greater and with new purpose, a path unseen suddenly becoming clearer, more importantly I was not alone as I walked away and when I paused to look back before driving away, I took notice that those I was leaving behind, well they were not alone either. It was time to start the journey of forgiving and understanding that folks are where they are, but we don't have to sit with them always. Sometimes the most loving thing we can do for others is to just walk away and pray that they soon come to know the truth and make the changes necessary for them.

It made me realize in my own ministry that there is no need for a leader for the maintenance of faith. The only need we have in learning and believing and growing is respect, for ourselves and for the diverse understandings of others. If you have been hurt by organized religion or a church family let me say to you now, "I AM SORRY YOU WERE HURT AND BETRAYED." I know you may never hear those words any other way. I am sorry people hurt or betrayed you and messed up your insides. If you have been a leader in the church caught up to do bidding that makes you uncomfortable, hand-picked and then abandoned by a priest after being convinced to do terrible things only to be thrown away, let me say to you now "I AM SORRY YOU WERE USED AND TOSSED ASIDE." I don't have all the answers to fix those kinds of hurts, but I am truly sorry for all people caught in such a mess as this. We are all fallible as humans, we make mistakes, we get sucked into group think, we are mean and short tempered. But those wounds, sometimes are an amazing opportunity for growth and understanding. There is no better way to healing then to be forged through the fires of pain into a stronger and better you. God does not just heal us through spiritual highs and well written books, but he sends us through storms and fires, floods and famines. We will always come out looking better then new.

So be courageous and strong and no that I am with you. Step up and stand out in your best you and when you cause a hurt fix it. Be brave, recognize your role, and fix it. Take ownership to your actions and change the outcome. You are today's action towards change and you can't make those changes while you're still sitting.

And Then There was COVID

WE are all wholly loving and wholly lovable

Since I have been working on this book and getting my ducks in a row, so to speak, to take larger steps toward a role within my beliefs, to be bolder as a minister, drastic changes have taken place around all of us. We live in a nation divided so extremely that we haven't even come together yet as neighbors to help each other through a pandemic. Businesses closing, people being requested to stay home and stay safe. Work has drastically shifted to a at home activity not allotting for a clear separation of living outside of the job. So, it only stands to reason that folks would ultimately start to twist things and proclaim their rights and freedoms and start to rebel against the safety of themselves and others, I mean really, that's what we do both as humans and Americans, is to complain about our rights if something suddenly, even if for the betterment of others and ourselves, changes or restricts our wants or lifestyles. We scream and holler and say it's a hoax or conspiracy. During these times of hardship, we find ministers and spiritual leaders using the current happenings as a way to fear folks into a place of belief and worship. They use the worlds/nations hardships for gain, to increase membership or income and these people forget and dismiss the huge responsibility to the soul's health and capacity to live free in times of immense struggle. That is not to say that all religious leaders are bad and wrong, many do the right thing, but those doing the right thing won't be incensed by this chapter. At the very heart of these times, we will always find diversity in our places of worship. Some houses of worship following the rules, some houses following the rule to the extreme like they may never open again and online will be the new way, and those that chose to stay open and encourage folks to come out joining in large groups to continue to praise God without fear... It is those folks, those leaders, choosing to stay open I am going address in the chapter, because fear manipulating fear does not belong in our houses of worship.

My mother and I speak every day, during this pandemic we began speaking to each other several times a day, talking about numbers and next steps, during the course of our conversations she had mentioned that her pastor was not going to shut down the church. Of course, we discussed the concerns with staying open. I gave her resources form CDC to share with the pastor and she was then told by the pastor during a weekly bible study, as things went along, that the church was going to close due to the governor's order. I was so relieved to hear this news. Turns out he did not close, and he really had no intention of listening to what any government official had to say. Which placed in him direct conflict with his own belief as a Christian. The bible states to follow the law of the land. The choices he was making, directly affected my family members and that gave me cause to question his motives. So, I did what I do, and I wrote a letter, talk about stepping up and stepping right into my next course, kicking and screaming all the way...

["Dear Pastor _____,

I am writing you today as a colleague. It is my understanding that you have chosen to keep the doors of your church open. God has not given us a spirit of fear but one of love, power, and a sound mind. You may be feeling anxious or fearful of the current circumstances

Dawn Feldman-Steis

as well as your congregants. I mean it is an invisible threat of harm to all of us. It is understandable also that a response to those fears would be, to stand in unison in faith as an action against the threats of harm around us, and to show this faith by keeping the doors open. Encouraging people to prove their faith by sacrificing their safety is NOT acting in love. If you have faith to move mountains and do not act in love it is nothing. Please, tell me where the love, power, and sound mind is, in keeping the doors open. To endanger the health of people as an act of faith in the face of fear is not acting in love. Knowingly endangering people to possible illness is not acting in love.

Just as God has placed a seed into the very core of a minister's soul so he has planted the seeds of health and safety into the souls of doctors and scientists. We are to bear witness to all of Gods servants and people. We have all been created for such a time as this… each of us having a role to play. With that being said, as ministers we have and obligation and responsibility to keep people both safe and edified. We keep people safe by heeding the warning of the doctors and scientists, as God has created them also for such a time as this. Have you considered the possible outcomes to your actions in keeping the doors open? People will get sick and when they do, they will either question their faith or feel like their faith wasn't enough. Maybe they will feel as if they didn't believe enough or haven't loved enough or haven't trusted in God to keep them safe and protected. But God sent the doctors and scientists to protect and give guidance and you are leading them away. What of the families of those that bear witness to folks getting ill or faith being testing in such a manner? We as ministers are charged with keeping folks spiritually healthy and prepared. Doctors are charged with keeping them physically healthy and prepared, we must work in tandem. Paul tells us that nothing is unclean unless we see it as unclean, but he warns that if what we do or say or act causes another to faulter or fall we are not acting in love, you are not loving your neighbors as yourselves.

I beg you to heed the warnings of those that God has prepared for such a time as this. I request that you recognize the gifts of everyone's spirit in these times as you look into the faces of Gods beloved and ask them to be diligent. If you personally feel a need to rise-up in actions of faith, do it in love. Start a call list for folks that chose not to come out. If folks are unable to get to the store, go shopping for them. Start a drive through prayer station that provides social distancing but encourages love and prayer. Encourage the other ministers in the church to make calls and keep prayers. Perform service online, provide the first virtual holy communion with folks. Just, please, close the doors both in an act of love and in an example of a sound mind so that all may come to know the sovereign power of God on the other side of this thing.

In Truth and Love always,

Rev. Dawn Marie Feldman-Steis"]

Now ask yourself, what is so bad in this letter that would generate enormous anger and hate. It always amazes me when I write letters, especially to ministers/ leaders, when they have a problem with it. They get so pissed off and I can't do anything but chuckle about it. They will preach sermons based on letters written by Paul to the churches, Paul a murderer of Christians and once very angry man, made saint and founder of the church and yet when someone writes to them according to a leading, today leaders become angry and judgmental. Yes, in the two weeks following the letter this Pastor did not take anytime to contact me or have any sort of adult conversation on his leading to stay open. The letter was sent privately, and he could have contacted me with his concerns privately. Instead during his sermons and rants, recorded online, he got angry, incredibly angry. He went on, in his sermons, about someone writing him and telling him he doesn't love his people... HIS people?! He at one point talked about he was not listening to anything that disrupted his peace and that if he wasn't at peace with what is being said it's not for him, more importantly it's not from God. How that peace translates to visible anger, well he will have to work through that himself. How many times have you been led to do something and had absolute peace about it? Most of the time I am being pushed towards acts of courage when I am led to act in my beliefs and guidance. As he talked, he escalated in his anger to a point in which he stated that the person speaking against his choice in staying open was listening to an angel of light. (For those that may not understand this description, this is an old school way of defining Satan or devils is that they come as an angel of light.) Oh my, yes he went there, back to that 80's Christian anger and fear and I just shook my head. He actually stumbled and stuttered when he said this, like he knew what he was about to say was so wrong and yet he said it anyway. That's what happens with displaced anger. I said while talking with my mother as we watched his meltdown on social media, I have done what I was led to do I can do nothing further, this Pastor is in God's hands now. Penny (Mom) then said I am waiting to hear him say, and I said wait for it here it comes... and BAM. Next thing out of his mouth is... IF you are not coming out to church and staying home you are operating in fear and against the will of god. And there it is... the threat of loosing your God by staying safe, by staying home. The seed of fear planted into the hearts and minds of the congregation. For what reason? Why? Money, fame, the show of it all? Pride maybe? No, I think it all played out that way for a larger more important reason and it goes something like this.

When this pastor became so angry with a simple letter, that could not really change anything he was doing with regard to leading his church, simply because no one knew about the letter but him. I began to pray, simply, "show me what I need to see in this. Tell me my next steps. Must I wage another battle with a church?" I began to see something under the surface, something hiding, yet very active in the shadows. It wasn't pride pushing this man or fame or just shitty leadership, it was fear. He was afraid the income of the church would dwindle in the middle of building a new church, he was afraid that folks would stop attending all together if they didn't keep coming weekly and he pushed his congregation into attending service by using fear to drive them to the alter all to ease his own personal fears of losing a building and income during this pandemic. He pitted their safety against their faith because his faith was failing. Can I just say... UNFUCKINGBELIEVABLE... There where so many other options then this, if he felt the need to be out and about why not check on his elderly shut ins, pray with those that would not leave the home, better the churches internet community and bring a larger group together online with the faith of bringing them to the church when things reopened. So many other answers then to put folks in harms way. But that's the way of fear, its blind and impulsive, its fight or flight response and it is what drives every co-dependent group. Fear is just a nasty business to handle or manipulate.

I made a comment about loving folks better and pointing out my disappointment online that day and then I was released from it all. I had completed my task and the rest was up to God. A few of the congregates of this church reached out to me after I had made my comment and asked some questions of me. They took an adult approach to what I was saying and questioned me. In talking with them I came to find out some other points of dissatisfaction within this particular church body. I found myself ministering to those that chose to stay home. They needed reassurance that they were not going to hell if they chose to stay home and stay healthy. In speaking with one young lady, she explained that she had some health concerns and when she had brought these concerns up in the past to this minister, he would tell her that her faith wasn't strong enough if she was struggling with health issues. If you need to go to the doctor for something it is a show of a lack of faith that God will heal you. She then explained that the minister said nothing about his own faith when he sought out an operation for a hernia and Lasik for his eyes. Those things seemed to be God ordained. I spent quite a bit of time encouraging and reaffirming to these folks that their faith was strong and intact and that they are wholly loving and wholly lovable in the eyes of God. In doing so my anger for the situation had turned its focus from addressing the pastor to assisting those harmed by the Pastors words. It also gave me some insight to underlying issues within this church community that could be addressed with the courage of a few parishioners stepping bravely into asking more pointed questions of this pastor. It gave me an area to continue in prayer for both this church and its leadership. Because what I know is that as surely as God places you in a place of leadership God reminds you that you are still a student.

So where to go from here? What is the next step when fear becomes so intertwined with our beliefs so much that faith is squeezed out of the picture all together? How do we learn to step away from fear baiting discussions and sermons within church walls and realign ourselves with faith and belief that is freeing to the soul's capacity to become consistently more? The dangerous part about listening to lectures and sermons that limit and diminish God, is that the head/mind is the trainer of the soul when we first start out. The head (our thoughts and knowledge) will keep our spirits from becoming and growing. The head needs to see to believe, needs to touch to know something, to smell to recognize something. Knowledge is power, yes, but only if that knowledge becomes knowable action within the spirit. It must become apart of the copilot in order to be operational in our lives, so it is with faith and belief. There is the knowledge of faith and belief and then there is knowing faith and belief. IF you truly know your faith, know your belief you automatically act in it. When I speak with Christians that I have known my whole life and see that they are exactly where they were in their knowledge 20 years ago and that knowledge continues to incapsulate God into a predisposed ideal of right and wrong, I am driven to rise up, driven to speak louder, to stay longer in places I never thought I would go.

I hate the conflict I feel when talking with some ministers; it's stressful and uneasy for me, but there is a bigger drive to correct the lies and myths that religion has used to bind people to pews and not purpose. There is a difference between pastoring a church and ministering to people. There shouldn't be but there is. All these things that I have talked about and more is why the worship centers and churches, mosques and synagogues have dwindled in their numbers. God is calling folks to be bigger than the walls of a church, to be up and in movement and not sitting in contentment and complacency. Jesus was in ministry, he walked among the people he went to them, and during this COVID pandemic we as ministers had an opportunity to be like Christ and go to the people, to step out and step up to a cause that would take us outside of the protected walls of church and provide aid and encouragement to those in need and many ministers failed in this call to be bigger than the church.

It is time that people understand that while you are sitting in that pew or chair in your house of worship waiting to hear the message, you should be built up to a point in which you are driven to give the message. You must become the minister to continue to hear and grow in the ministry you feel within yourself. If you have been sitting in a house of worship for more than two years and have not yet preached or given a sermon then you are in the wrong place. You are the leaders to your faith, not a minister or pastor, you are the reason the faith is there, the reason the belief goes on. You are the creation of God, formed and made to create and grow endlessly both in this world and the next. It is time to take ownership to who you are and who you have been created to be. If you hear something that hits wrong question it, if you are placed in a position to fear and not act in faith question it, if you see others being harmed or gossiping as a weapon question it, you are responsible to your own growth as well as the growth of the person sitting next to you and you have the permission and right to question leadership and to encourage your own ministry and next steps within your house. And church is your house. As soon as you place any amount of donation into that pate, basket, or bin you became a share holder to that business. You are stake holder and your ideas and questions, concepts and imaginings count to the whole of the business plan. I am asking you to take ownership, ownership of the things you have said and left unsaid, done and left undone. Be brave, step in faith away from fear and trust that what God has told you is important to your neighbor, become the minister, set yourself as equal and watch growth happen. The church as a building is owned by the people in it, you are no guest in these houses you are the reason the house was built. Take ownership of the labels you hold within yourself and strive to create more. I am passionate about the pain that the church can cause, and it takes bold brave steps to correct it. I want nothing more than all of the abuse within church walls to stop. The church has abused their power for years in everyway imaginable and it is truly time that the folks attending address this. Its starts by asking questions of your leaders and yourself. Something I have recognized during this pandemic is that the more I sit in this house more I want to sit. The less I move the less I want to move... It is the same with belief, the more we know in the spirit the more the spirit wants to know. The more knowledge we take in the more we seek knowledge.

Just a thought here. Have you ever been in a place within your church that feels off, like you may not be alone, like that sixth sense thing goes off and you feel as though the church itself is haunted? Or that room is unsettled, or you don't want to walk the hall alone? Maybe its not so much the souls left behind but the souls that have been hurt with in those walls, both the living and the dead. Energy leaves a mark and traces in dark corners. The anguish we cause each other lingers and become spiritual goo for others coming in and out and it leaves a stain on us and the walls. I am setting course to call folks to clean up the goo in our churches as well as ourselves. That which we have seen happen does not need to happen again. That what we have participated in or not participated in does not continue to define our faith or beliefs. That recognizing our responsibility to question one another drives us to see our need to apologize to each other and to forgive each other and by doing so brings us closer to our creator. Knowing the creator teaches the soul to imagine greater and bigger and bolder ideas, the soul not the mind, when the soul is empowered and finds growth then the ideas

Dawn Feldman-Steis

within creation expand, so does our capacity to become. I want us to stop sitting and I want us all to become., become all these things and more just as Jesus said.

To all my ministering friends reading. WE must stop looking at questions as judgment. WE must stop defining those that step courageously to question us as troublemakers and not suited for this place of worship. WE are not here to guide people out the doors but rather to raise them up to such a level that they go willing into the day, week and next stage of their lives in the grace and mercy of an ever changing and growing world as leaders and independently strong within or without the church. Mahammad, Buddha, Jesus, all the prophets before and in this moment have a ministry and we are all prophets all ministers to our convictions and beliefs. All the great leaders believe in something greater than themselves, something outer worldly that touches only the souls of mankind. I call that collective thought of something larger GOD and in this knowledge of all beliefs having a god we learn to know, GOD in all of the forms through out all of this world as living breathing ever growing God. We must minister to everyone and all of creation. This notion of elitism of a belief or religion being "the right belief" or "the only way" must stop being apart of the course. If we subscribe to the idea of omni potent within our beliefs of God, then we must recognize how vast that belief is and stop boxing the message and love into neat little boxes with just a piece of the whole never giving out the whole. Once we as ministers truly accept a god that is god to all of creation the need to fear people into the pews leaves, the desire to elevate yourself to maintain your position leaves, and true work and mission will begin with the church and more importantly the folks sitting in them. As ministers we have an obligation to work within your beliefs, but it is a privilege to share and speak with those listening. You are not in charge of the people; the people must be your guide. The biggest sermon you will ever give to folks is the one that gives people the permission to love GOD intimately, consistently so that they may know how much they are genuinely loved in the same way. Stop shutting folks down and supervising the organization of church and give them a reason to step up and step forward into individual belief. I say this to myself as much as I say it to you as ministers, we should be opening the doors to let folks out walking in confidence to their ministries, not to bring folks in and keep them there. We need to give the options to let folks out of their fears and strong holds to give a truthful opportunity to independently live with and in a presence of God. I am talking about giving folks permission... permission to step outside of the mindset and put the soul in charge.

Permission is an interesting concept when it comes to beliefs. I remember having a conversation with a friend after a service. We got into a discussion about the possibility of preaching a sermon from the Books of Enoch. I stated that it is important that we seek out other holy texts left out of the whole. That we should be sharing and encouraging each other to study more than what we have. He came back and said, "yes I study those things I look into them but these folks in church can barely handle the 66 books of the bible and learning them, how could we possibly introduce anything more?" I stepped back a bit, we stood in silence for a moment and then I said, "but how did they learn about the 66 books of the bible, how did they know of it? How do any of us know about any of the books we read or study? Because we have been told, we have been shown and these things have been talked about. How can we expect folks to be encouraged to have permissions if we have a mindset that dictates, they can't handle more than just 66 books of a bible?" He said, "we can't give them this information it is just not the right time," and then he walked away. It was in this moment I realized that ministers should have term limits, so to speak. Our houses of worship should have more than one lead and those leaders should rotate and change and those in attendance should be a part of that rotation, uplifted and encouraged to step up and outside of their norm and our norm and into a more soulful stance toward belief. Imagine a worship center that creates ministers and allows ministers to remain excited in the actions of love and being loved.

I get excited when I see the possibility of the soul's capacity as endless. Wouldn't it be an amazing day to see a house of worship that had a rotation of beliefs and leaders from all practices in faith. A place that truly accepted everyone, always.

Becoming the Calling

"Tell Them I AM that I AM sent you."
NKJV

I wrote this book as a journey of self-healing and an act toward forgiveness. It started as a way to take back my stories that had been manipulated through gossip that was driven by hate. This has given me some empowerment in a powerless journey of healing. The second reason for writing this book is that I know that I am not the only person that has gone through pain in their worship centers. There is a large group of us that have thrown the idea of spiritual community away because of the actions of a few. Outside of the glaring issues within the churches regarding abuse with children, there are sneakier and more derisive issues within the walls that need to be addressed. Keeping folks in a spiritual prison, by way of using their worst fears against them, must end. The isolation and mistreatment of people, because they dare to take a stand or question leadership, must end. Placing folks into categories that deny them an opportunity for promotion to leadership positions, must end. It is time we begin the process of creating a community of worship that generates independent thought and growth. We must stop sitting. The abuse behind the walls must stop, and starts with those of us who are, and have been paying attention.

The day I walked out of that church, after being trapped in a room and berated by vestry members, after being bullied by a priest for six months, I felt so free. I felt God had released me from staying in this worship center. My spirit could finally rest, and by the afternoon I felt this satisfaction of peace returning. I had been fighting just to stay the course for the last six months, and the journey was rugged and hard. I was tired both mentally and spiritually. Walking away, letting go and knowing that I was truly letting go of it all with my best efforts made was a wonderful release. I didn't have to worry about the what ifs and what's next. I would not be returning, and I felt as if I had done everything I could to encourage a different thought, a different way. I contacted a few friends that evening and talked a bit about what had happened; that it was finally over. I was, as they say, "Brushing the dirt from my feet."

The next morning, about 7:30, I was reading a book with a cup of Joe and the doorbell rang. I stood up and looked around the corner and an officer was standing at my door. I did a double take, as I am the mother of a young man who recently moved away and joined the army. The sight of the officer sent crazy fears through me. The first thing I thought was my son had been harmed, or something terrible had happened to a family member. The doorbell rang again snapping me back into the now and away from my current thoughts. I went to the door. The young officer asked my name and explained that I was being served and must appear in court tomorrow. He handed me paperwork and explained that if I wanted to make a counter complaint I could do so at the local sheriff's office. He left and I went back to the table. I began to look through the complaint. It was a stay order filed by "the priest" of the church.

There went that peace, that sense of a project finished.

Suddenly I was entering a new chapter, one that would prove to be a lengthy journey. After a long rant of extended cuss words and a few phone calls I began to really read through what this woman had written. She handwrote descriptions of me with accusations of threatening her after she refused to accept a glass of wine, that I texted her and stated I would call her out during a sermon. This

Dawn Feldman-Steis

was grossly twisted to what really happened six months ago, and not yesterday. She made check marks on the harassment box and the misuse of electronic communication box. There was something written in about trespassing. That's funny now, simply because a member of the church cannot really be trespassing if they are there for church, right? I began to see that there were several questions one must answer when completing a form such as this. Did the accused threaten you with harm? She said no. Did they commit dating violence or sexual assault against you? She said no. Has the individual stalked or attempted to stalk you? Again, she said no. Have you felt threatened or in fear of being harmed or even killed by this person? Yet again, she said no. She wrote a narrative of allegations that she has been relaying over the course of a six-month period, yet when asked to prove any of it she fell short.

The peace order was eventually dismissed but there was more fire for me to walk through, as the process of being found innocent was a modern day play out of the Jesus story all over again, and I got to sit in a leading role.

I had to find an attorney in one day to go to court the next day. I had a few friends help with that and contacted an attorney, scheduled a meeting and went over my case in less than four hours, only to be told that the attorney himself would not be able to attend and I would have to go into court for the first time in my life, alone. He told me to go in and request a final hearing, as my attorney was unable to attend that day, that I was to state that I was not guilty. He then said that the judge would schedule a future date for trial and at that date, the case would be thrown out. I left feeling somewhat better but terrified that I would be going into court alone. My friend Cimone called as I was driving home from the attorney's office. I told her what had happened and what was next for me. She again, just like the trip to Fairmont, popping up as if ordained by God, said she would be to my home in the morning, and she would go with me. It helped take the edge off, but I still felt unprepared and alone.

I went to bed that night rerunning the events of the last six months over and over in my head. The accusations she made, all these terrible lies, haunted me. Never was she questioned, by the leaders of the church, to show proof or substantiate her claims. I realized and came to understand that this was a woman so wrapped up in herself, to the extent that the lies she had told put her in a position with which she had no other option than to continue the narrative. And those around her believed the story so deeply, in her fabricated turmoil, that they insisted she pursue this fully. She had to keep the small white lie that started in Jan going as it had gotten so large that even she could not back out of it, unless she just busted and told the truth, and at this point what would the truth cost her? And what does her lie really cost me?

I showed up to court. She had her people strategically around her, all old friends I once considered to be my family. There I was, one friend off to the side, trying to face the situation with calm and courage. When we stood before the first judge, I said my lines: My attorney is not present, and I am not guilty, and I request a final trial date. I felt like I repeated them six or seven times before the judge accepted my request and scheduled a date for trial. During the scheduling for the trial "the Priest" was asked to give an account of the events that she felt justified her actions. Things she said didn't happen in her initial narrative, she then alluded to in court, verbally. I suppose she had an audience to appease. As she talked, she took every story, every email in confidence, and used them in the proceeding. At one point she suggested that I might be using drugs, fully knowing I was in recovery. She also felt I made sexual advances toward her, not really knowing my status, and said that I made a scene at the church, never mentioning that it was church members who pulled me into a room. I, of course, remained silent. I just stood there, alone, before the priest and the people that used to embrace me as part of the family and could say nothing. As I stood there and listened, I realized that the lies and the scene playing out looked like the crucifixion of Christ. I realized that the physical pain of the crucifixion was not the worst of it, that even the betrayal of friends, was not the worst of it. The worst thing of the crucifixion was the absolute isolation. As I listened and stood before the judge, I wasn't thinking what I could say to this, I already was told to say nothing. I wasn't thinking about how to defend myself. All I could think about was the isolation Jesus must have felt before Pontius pilot as the priests and rabbis, who praised him days before, stood trial against him, and how he stood quietly still and said nothing. How that isolation must have followed him throughout the process of his death as one of his deepest wounds.

We scheduled the next trial date a month later, only prolonging the pain of it all. I proceeded to the clerk's office to acquire a recording of the proceedings for my attorney, and a bit for myself. A month later the trial proved no wrong on my part and the order and charges were dismissed and denied by the court. The judge felt the courts to be misused and no merit to the claims and shut it down. I was free to go. All this was played out to cement her lie into the minds of the congregates attending.

And yet, as I waited for that second trial to take place, I found myself pissed off all the time. I was so angry that I had stepped back into a church community, again, only to be persecuted and mistreated. I had spent eight years with these folks, and they had not heard one word of my side to the story—not one person asked. Everyone blindly followed the testimony of the leader because of the uniform she wore, and not the knowledge they had of both parties involved. I was super pissed at God, as I now felt set up and abandoned yet again. I have struggled with that anger on and off until recently. I finally gave it some time. I was meditating one morning and said to myself that I missed feeling joyful. Where had my joy gone? As I thought about it, I talked about it. Finally, one evening while driving, I just let it go and questioned God as to why he would allow such a fantastic mess to come about when I was returning to church. Why, after allowing me to fall in love with a creator would I be left at the altar? I railed on it for a good hour or so. I reran, almost daily, things that had been said to me while being trapped in a room unable to get out, all the while watching this "possessed" priest whisper into someone's ear, while staring at me, telling a person what to say next. It was on constant loop, nagging and haunting me every day. It was slowly becoming maddening and there appeared to be some sort of PTSD forming in the middle of it all. As I fought through these memories and pondered things over and over for the next several months I prayed and read as much as I could regarding forgiveness and healing. I have always been an instant forgiver. I can forgive and move on from something with a snap of the fingers. I don't hold on like this. But here I was, my spirit trapped away from the journey because my mind was stuck on a loop. I was attempting to sleep one evening, and as I tossed and turned, I sat straight up and said, "WHAT?! What am I missing in all this? Why can't I let this shit go?" Then the spirit said just as easy as a light wind whispered, "Because you love them."

WHAT?! The problem wasn't that I hated, or that I was angry. The problem was that I was hurt because I loved them, and more importantly, I love them still, as they were family to me for as long as my stay at the church. The spirit was saying, "You can't be hurt and betrayed, mopped up and thrown away if you don't love them. None of what has happened matters if you don't love them." Mind blown, I stayed up that night with this new thought. It was true, I was hurt and stuck on replay, not because of the damage done to me but because of the love I held for them. That love was in constant contradiction to my anger and the reason I felt no joy. The next day I woke and pondered what to do about all this. I meditated and decided that even if I didn't feel it, I knew it was what was happening. I began my meditation that day by saying each name out loud, followed by, I love you. "Priest, I love you. Kit, I love you. Junior and Senior, I love you." And so on. The first run through the list of names was rough but I have done this every time my mind goes back to those days, and though it has been a few years, I have only just started to heal. When I get trapped in reliving my days with that church, I just run through my list and declare the love I have and will continue to maintain for my once church family. Within the hour I am filled with joy, and the course is set. Among the core characteristics of co-dependency is an excessive reliance on other people for approval and a sense of identity. I had become co-dependent in my position and relationships, in the church. I began to see that love after the fire was going to lead me to peace and healing, and it has. This is what I call becoming and independent Episcopalian.

You see, co-dependence confiscates your permissions, and by doing so limits your capacity to be more, to be all these things around you and more. It steals away the I AM declarations in your life, it dictates sameness amongst the group, and that being likeminded or in the same condition is the right way. It creates religious bondage by limiting us within its walls and traditions. God provides endless opportunity without any limitation. So, our houses of worship coupled with our belief in God have become like oil and water, and create constant conflict between the mind and the soul. Consider the idea that independent faith does not come from what we are able to do or the abilities we have; but a recognition that independence comes from our knowing, truly knowing, what we are capable of. Independence is daring to explore; in doing so we begin to recognize the freedom in our ability to change within those capacities. It's not what we are able to do but what we are capable of doing through creation and our imaginations ability to create. Through these imaginings we take off the locks of our minds, allowing us freedom to believe that all these things and more are GOD. Defining and redefining, refining and melting down, and refining again is the most natural way of being next to God. A constant state of creation with endless capacity to do so becomes the simplest statements of love. Let's not seek love in the face of God, but let's act in love toward those that have been placed on our paths. That was the course set for me by my church family. In their actions they created a clear path for me to step up and take on the role of pastor. The Hounds of Heaven have nothing on the manipulative ways of a church congregation.

We all have great success in our lives, and your best effort is your best effort; it's easy to own all our right/correct choices. We should share those things that work for us, and bring us to the next level. We must also take ownership of those failures in our lives. The things that didn't work out. Sometimes we just need to try again, and sometimes we need to walk away. No matter the outcome to any new idea or imagining we must remain the owner of the outcome. In our lives it is inevitable that we will hurt others and others will hurt us. By taking ownership in our role, we gain a form of independence in growth and learning. Taking possession of these actions allows us to see them and look at them, and allows us growth in the process of knowing the truth, and allowing the truth to be enough. We no longer need to embellish our worst pains and fears, there is no competition to our struggles. I wonder what God would have done in the Garden of Eden if Adam and Eve had taken ownership over their choice and not passed it off as being someone else's fault? Forgiveness is like a spiritual heartbeat, a soul's muscle so to speak. We must exercise it to keep the soul healthy.

I was recently having a conversation with my photographer. We were discussing trees and the spiritual importance of them in our lives, and our different viewpoints of a tree and their true magnificence. Trees have always been a point of connection for me. Just standing in the forest on a breezy day listening to them sway and moan, branches knocking about is spiritual revelation to me. I also continue to see God as a big tree, always have, always will. As I was explaining this, this photographer looked at me and said, "I get it, I love trees myself. What's really cool about a tree is that they know when to lay down." There was brief pause as I took that nugget of info in. What she said stayed with me as I headed to my next appointment. What an immensely profound statement. "A tree knows when to lay down." Storms come and go but a tree, it still stands tall and proud, constantly creating and becoming, keeping a record of changes in its core, and when the time comes, the tree makes a conscious decision to lift its roots and lie down, to become again new and changed giving back to where it began. Doesn't this analogy just sum it all up, doesn't that just say it all. It's time for those of us that have been hurt by the church and our places of worship to pick up our roots, lie down, and be the conscious choice by becoming the ministry in the church. Stepping back into our houses of worship with new insights and supported by a different foundation. Step up and sit next to the person being spoon fed and encourage them to want more. Those you see sitting ask them to stand with you. Those that have a message to share, make a way for them to share it. Question the leaders, and their understandings as much as you question yourselves. Those hurt by the church share a common understanding. We can use our journeys to become the active ministry within the walls. We can become the true rotation of love in creations circles, and in a moment's notice, we are reminded of the innocence of our spirit. That's what I have been doing through all these stories, becoming the calling that was set out for me since I was a child. As you sit in peace, closing your eyes to breath in and out, listening further still, can you hear the soul whispering? Because I can, and it says: "Now Let's Begin..."